Five Steps To Better Multi-language Programming Using Metrics

Simplicity In Multi-language Coding: C/C++, Java, Bash, and Python

The Path To Better-Quality Software

2nd Edition

Stephen B. Morris

Table of Contents

Copyright

Five Steps To Better Multi-language Programming
Using Metrics, 2nd Edition

Copyright © 2018 by Stephen B. Morris

Paperback Edition

Dedication

This book is dedicated to Siobhan, as always.

Introduction

About This Book

This book is about software development simplicity. Why is there a need for consideration of simplicity in software development? Isn't modern software development now simply a case of dreaming up a solution and then magically the code gets written? Given that it's now commonplace to read newspaper articles about journalists writing an app in a day, have we not reached the promised land of software where code can be written on demand by pretty much anyone with a laptop or a smart phone? Hasn't the problem of the production of code been solved?

Unfortunately, the answer to these questions is a resounding no. While it's laudable that there is so much interest in software development - specifically coding - there is a tendency to trivialise what is in fact a tough discipline. Even professionals struggle to produce good code. Indeed, many organizations are engaged in what might be described as a life and death struggle to manage their software products and services and to map the future course of their work.

There is a growing range of devices in common use. This includes laptops, smart phones, tablets, and many other gadgets. Proficiency in using these devices is just that - proficient use. This is not a substitute for being able to build software for such devices.

It may well be feasible for a complete novice to attend an expensive day course and, with a lot of help, to then produce a really basic app. However, this bears very little resemblance to the efforts required to engage in day-to-day professional programming. Unfortunately, the ubiquitous nature of software technology seems to have given rise to a notion that, with a little effort, anybody can write code. This is a dangerous idea.

Aside from a complete beginner taking a short course to produce code, there's also the case of a slightly more savvy non-developer who downloads a trial copy of a package and runs some of the canned examples. In both of these cases, the non-professional can appear to be quite knowledgeable. Even politicians are getting involved - peppering their press interviews with comments about the growing need to teach school children about coding. Perhaps it is gradually dawning on journalists, politicians, and other commentators that there is a difference between using technology and creating technology. However, it is important that we don't make the mistake of trivialising software development.

The fact remains that non-professionals taking day courses and discussing coding has very little to do with proper software development as it's practiced by the many thousands of dedicated professional programmers around the world. Producing good-quality code day in and day out is a demanding job. All the more so, considering the fast pace of change in the IT world. In short, software development is a difficult craft.

This begs the question: Why should software development be easy? Any worthwhile craft is generally difficult to learn and practice effectively. To illustrate this, take the case of plumbing. One doesn't see journalists talking about how easy it is to install an electric shower in a day! I guess the reason why software (rather than plumbing) is seen as a desirable learn-in-a-day enterprise is because so many of us routinely use software technology.

Indeed, the ubiquity of software technology perhaps implies that it must therefore be easy to produce that technology. It's possibly natural (if a little odd) for non-practitioners to assume that software development is easy. This is simply not the case. Software development is a difficult craft.

One of the reasons for writing this book is that I believe there is a compelling argument in favour of simplicity in software development. We'll get into how this can be achieved later on, but for the moment it's important to remember that software now pervades just about every part of society. One might even say that software is now in the DNA of society.

One can't book a plane ticket without using the Web. Also, many government services can now only be accessed using websites. Online banking is increasingly widely used. Whole music collections can now reside in the cloud. The same is true for personal email, photos, videos, documents, and so on. All of this is powered by software technology.

If I could sum up this book's raison-d'etre in one sentence: **The need for solid design and good simple code has never been greater.**

The Takeaways From This Book

The following are some of the skills and ideas that I hope readers will take away.

Takeaway #1: Metric-driven coding

What are metrics? Metrics are simple rules that allow programmers, reviewers, and managers to look at code and determine the quality of that code. Metrics provide a way for programmers to stand back from their code and examine it with "another pair of eyes". In other words, metrics allow for a useful means of code self-review. The action of standing back and reviewing can help in avoiding a great many errors and can also help in raising the quality of the code before it gets checked back into the version control system.

The best kinds of metrics are those that can be self-administered by the coder. I'll introduce a comprehensive set of such metrics.

We'll see that the use of metrics provides for a really nice iterative model of coding. In addition, there is no reason why metrics cannot be used by managers to look at the quality of the code being produced. Also, software tools could easily be written to automatically extract metric data and the results can be published in intraweb reports or in other continuous integration artifacts. Indeed, many organizations are already using tools such as these to provide some checks on code quality.

Takeaway #2: The ability to read and understand existing code

It is extremely important to be able to read code written by others. Given that we are now in an era of multiple languages, it is more challenging than ever to understand legacy code. The reason for this is down to the growing range of platforms, tools, and technologies. Metrics provide some simple rules for surviving in the ever richer IT landscape.

Takeaway #3: The ability to design and write safe code

Many programmers are excellent at writing brand new code. However, design is often neglected and this generally is reflected in the quality of the finished code. The global adoption of agile techniques may well have reduced the amount of time spent on software design. In other words, it is possible that on many projects, coding may be starting too soon. This rush to coding is often at the expense of good design all because of the demands of agile sprints.

Takeaway #4: The ability to modify existing code

We all want to write new code. But, there's a lot of code already out there. Maintaining existing code is an extremely valuable skill. A key part of modifying legacy code is not breaking it or breaking other code that depends on it. Clearly, understanding the code is crucial before changing it.

Takeaway #5: Case studies illustrating design and working code

Rather than just talking about coding, I include many multi-language code examples illustrating the principles of design and metric-driven coding practices. Remember, metrics are simply rules that good programmers follow all the time. This translates into best practice, which in turn, generally results in better code.

What happens when there are no metrics in use?

High-quality code is a wonderful thing. It works and works well. Such code is changeable, well-tested, and well-designed. Poor-quality code on the other hand is different. It's usually a bit ugly, hard to understand, poorly tested, and unlikely to stand up to review or downstream changes.

How often have you come across code that looks okay but starts to reveal its unpleasant secrets as the project unfolds or (worse) in production? This is particularly true of concurrent coding. Badly written concurrent code can pass all the development tests, but may suddenly and inexplicably fail under heavy loading in production.

The absence of a metrics-driven development approach is usually pretty obvious. Projects that limp from one crisis to the next are sometimes a clear indicator that all is not well. How often have you seen reams of complex code that has:

1. Little or no unit testing
2. No functional tests
3. Memory leaks

4. Sloppy file handling
5. Sloppy database connection handling
6. Uncontrolled recursion exhausting stack space

> Fixing such problems can be a laborious exercise in adding logging code, modifying the source code, writing tests, adding more logging, etc. In effect, reversing the usual coding process. It is far more satisfactory to simply design, write, and test the code correctly in the first place. A metric-driven approach helps avoid poor practices.

Judging a Project in progress

> At the beginning of a project, have you ever been handed a set of project guidelines that reads something like the following:

1. This project will be finished way ahead of schedule
2. No design documents are to be produced - in the modern era, coding is the same as design
3. No effort is to be invested in developing or integrating any logging facilities
4. Design patterns are to be used only insofar as such patterns reside in the open source products chosen for the project
5. All code is to be optimized from the word go
6. Code modularization and general tidying up will be done in a separate downstream project
7. Minimal effort is to be expended on test facilities - end users are there to test developer code
8. No effort is to be directed into automated testing
9. Etc.

The resulting software from such a project is usually a pretty disastrous monstrosity. The lack of a coherent design often means that there is no vision for the finished system. Such projects are typically plagued with technical coding difficulties and developers may struggle throughout because of a lack of any meaningful design or coding guidelines. There is a better way.

Low quality code causes problems downstream. It really is true that the quicker you start to code, the longer the project is going to take.

A distillation of real-world tools and techniques - the four S's

This book is a distillation of some useful multi-language software development techniques derived from many years of experience in a wide range of environments. The emphasis is on what might be called the four S's. That is, programming for code **safety, security, simplicity, and survivability**.

Code safety

Code **safety** is a highly desirable attribute because safe code runs in an economical manner carefully managing its allocated resources. Safe code requests system resources, such as, file handles, memory, network access, and so on and makes efficient use of those resources before correctly returning them to the system. If problems occur during execution, safe code tries to handle itself in the best manner possible, e.g., logging exceptions and failing gracefully. Here's a small example of code safety in C++ in Listing 1.

Listing 1 - Unsafe C++ code
```
ABigClass* a = new ABigClass();
ABigClass* b = new ABigClass();
a = b; // Memory leak
```

In Listing 1, I allocate two instances of a C++ class and I then erroneously assign one to the other. What could be simpler? Is there a problem with Listing 1? Believe it or not, the code in Listing 1 has the power to potentially bring the largest server to its knees. This is simply because the memory allocated to the first object is not returned to the system. If this code runs in a continuous loop, where the two allocations happened many times, then the memory leakage could become critical. I know this because, a few years ago, I wrote a piece of C++ code that had just such a memory leak. The code ran continuously and eventually the host system ran out of memory. This was a tough problem to solve.

Later, we'll see how the use of metrics can help in avoiding this type of situation.

Another example of unsafe code in C rather than C++ is illustrated in Listing 2.

Listing 2 More unsafe code – this time in C
```
char* textString;
textString = malloc(256);

// Lots more code in here

free(textString);
```

In Listing 2, we have a memory allocation followed by a de-allocation with some intervening code. Surely, there's no big issue with this code? Unfortunately, Listing 2 is also unsafe for the simple reason that it makes an assumption that the call to `malloc` always succeeds. The code works just fine as long as that assumption remains true. However, if the `malloc` fails (as it might do if free memory is low), then the result of the call to `free` is undefined. You really don't want your code to enter into undefined territory. The results are completely undefined, e.g., it might result in de-allocating a random block of memory.

Code security

Code **security** is another highly desirable attribute. Given that hundreds of billions of dollars are lost every year to cybercriminals, it is essential that code be made as secure as possible. Have a look at the code in Listing 3 and see do you think it's secure.

Listing 3 Potential security problem code

```
int main ()
{
   char str1[6] = { 's', 't', 'r', 'i', 'n', 'g' };
   char str2[30];
   strcpy (str2, str1);
   puts (str1);
   puts (str2);

   return 0;
}
```

Such a small amount of code and yet it contains a potentially catastrophic problem. Why? Well, it's in the call to `strcpy`. This relies on the presence of a null terminator at the end of `str1`. If the null terminator is missing (as it is in this case), then the copy operation will continue until a null character is located in RAM or until a memory protection fault occurs. Not good and definitely not secure.

Code simplicity

Code **simplicity** is often overlooked in our multi-language era. How often have you looked at reams of unstructured JavaScript or Python code that is practically impenetrable? And don't forget the addition of Ajax to the mix.

Enterprise end users increasingly demand highly responsive front ends that are characteristic of desktop applications and Web-based utilities. This end user demand makes a strong case for using Ajax with the attendant coding complexity. The mixture of programming languages helps to fulfil the requirements, but this is at the expense of complex source code.

Subscribing to simplicity means ensuring that designs are clean and crisp. If recourse must be made to complex language features, then decent documentation should be provided to help the next programmer in line to maintain the code.

Listing 4 is an example of what looks like quite complex Java code. We'll review this code later on, but for now I note that, from a refactoring point of view, the addition of some comments might make it easier to understand.

Listing 4 Complex-looking code from Java 8
```
public static void main(String... args) {
   Calculator myApp = new Calculator();
```

```
IntegerMath addition = (a, b) -> a + b;
IntegerMath subtraction = (a, b) -> a - b;
RealMath division = (a, b) -> a / b;
System.out.println("137 / 12 = " +
   myApp.operateBinary(137, 2, division));
System.out.println("40 + 2 = " +
   myApp.operateBinary(40, 2, addition));
System.out.println("20 - 10 = " +
   myApp.operateBinary(20, 10, subtraction));
}
```

We'll see many examples of how to write simpler code.

Code survivability

Coding for **survivability** means looking down the road beyond the current project and trying to ensure that your code will have a good chance of running on future platforms and even co-existing with the languages of the future. For example, if a given piece of C++ code leaks memory then that may have an unpredictably bad effect if the code is called from another language such as Python or Java. In other words, survivable code doesn't rely on the runtime system to clean up after bad programming.

Listing 5 illustrates an example of Java code with poor survivability. Why?

Listing 5 Code with poor survivability
```
try {
    // Java code here
    // Some more code that could throw an exception
    // More Java code
} catch (Exception anException) {
    anException.printStackTrace();
}
```

Well, the problem with Listing 5 lies in the fact that the exception handler doesn't actually do anything meaningful with the exception beyond printing it out. In general, once an exception occurs, the code has become partly unstable and this needs to be corrected. Just printing an exception is not sufficient and while the code in Listing 5 may pass all the programming tests, it represents a negative investment. The outcome of such a negative investment is pain for the users and the unfortunate maintainer.

Another commonly used version of the Listing 5 code is omitting a catch clause and just using a finally clause. This has the same effect of not handling the exception with the result that the code may be de-stabilised. A further note to this topic is that Java 9 intends to deprecate `finally` clauses because they are potentially non-deterministic.

Code in the real world

I think it's fair to say that complexity is seen as a desirable code attribute by some programmers. I can recall years ago reading code comments that were something like: "Only real programmers will understand this code". The comment was then followed by some incomprehensible code involving regular expressions, bit shifting, masking, etc. all with no documentation whatsoever. This type of practice is deeply counterproductive. The result is bad code, which may work today but if nobody but the original author understands it, then it is code that diminishes in value over time.

Have you experienced asking an author of some excessively complex code how that code works? All too often, they quickly forget how their code works. This makes for unnecessary difficulties if such code has to be changed in the future. So, it's far better for everyone if code is kept simple.

This is all the more true today as programmers struggle to code in multiple languages. Keeping it simple is no longer a choice but a necessity.

Why Multiple Languages?

Why have I decided to use multiple languages in the book? The main reason for this is that the bulk of modern enterprise software development now involves more than one language. For example, a common combination of languages is Java, CSS, HTML, JavaScript, and SQL. Another popular language set is C++, Java, Python, CSS, HTML, and JavaScript. Added to the language mix is the use of frameworks, such as Spring, Struts, Play, etc.

Map-reduce frameworks, such as Hadoop, are also growing in popularity. The same is true for the growing use of NoSQL database technology, such as MongoDB. In parallel with this, programming is becoming ever more complex.

The plethora of languages in common use is an even more compelling reason to embrace coding simplicity. This is because downstream programmers may not have the same programming language skills as the original coders. The latter can occur where programming is passed to an offshore company. So, it's better if the original programmers try to keep it simple.

Also, many organizations utilize a range of languages for strategic reasons, e.g., the aggressive use of JavaScript can help to extend the lifespan of core servers. In this context, for intraweb applications, business logic can be pushed all the way out to the browser by making use of advanced JavaScript libraries. While this is understandable, it is also a strategy that contains some risk, e.g., the JavaScript libraries may not be stable or they may be very complex to program. Also, some JavaScript libraries may exhibit strange behaviour in certain browsers. There's no such thing as free technology and the end result of unnecessarily mixing so many languages and technologies may be very complex code.

What all languages have in common is the scope for poorly crafted code. A central theme of this book is that low quality code results in weak products, diminishes the reputation of programmers as well as the reputation of the organization. The industry badly needs the implementation of robust multi-language solutions and this topic is the core of this book.

Debunking some myths

The IT industry is now global and is not without its very own mythology. I'll therefore take the opportunity to debunk some popular myths and to give my own take on what I consider are some dangerous practices. Perhaps the most dangerous practice of all is that of perpetuating the myth that programming is easy.

I'm sometimes a little puzzled when I read about some of the sincere efforts to teach, in a day or two, the craft of programming to complete beginners. Of course, we all have to start somewhere, but it simply isn't feasible to produce an expert programmer in a matter of days. An example of this are the so-called coding dojos that go to schools. These groups are usually headed up by volunteers and exist to try to impart the skills of programming to school children.

The dojos often use Python as the language of choice because this is a language that has a lightweight setup and is relatively easy to get up and running. While the coding dojo intention is undoubtedly good, trying to teach such a deeply technical skill as programming in a highly condensed timeframe is likely to have poor results. I wonder in years to come will some ex-pupils look back on these coding dojos with the same lack of nostalgia usually reserved for poorly taught mathematics courses? Again, coding is just one aspect of software development. You can't build a house without a foundation.

This brings us neatly to our first myth.

Myth #1: Coding is easy.

As will become clear soon, good coding is decidedly not easy. When you get it right, coding is very rewarding. But, it's definitely not easy. Very often, there exists a multiplicity of ways of getting code wrong and only one or two ways of getting it right. Just because it works or appears to work, doesn't mean it's right. This will become clearer when we look at some code examples.

Myth #2: The ability to read code is no longer a relevant skill

This might be called 'write-and-forget' and is a dangerous approach. I've often looked at indecipherable code. In some cases, I've been tasked with changing such code to add a new feature or to make some other modification. Getting started is usually a very laborious exercise in adding logging, running the code, making some simple changes, adding more logging, etc. If, on the other hand, the code is clearly written to begin with then subsequent changes are much easier to achieve.

I recall one example of a particularly incomprehensible piece of JavaScript code and I asked the original author how it worked. Sadly, the author said he didn't know and had long since forgotten even writing the code. There was no design document, just reams of code. Adding the new code proved to be a less than rewarding and unnecessarily time-consuming experience.

The ability to read other people's code confers a significant advantage on a programmer. This is a particularly useful skill when dealing with indecipherable code.

Myth #3: Project planning is not needed with agile development

It's generally been my experience that the most successful software is also the best-planned software. In other words, spending time on content planning is nearly as important as design and coding. Unfortunately, this contention runs completely counter to the thinking in a lot of organizations. Very often, there is a misconception that an agile approach obviates the need for careful development planning. Agile development is not a replacement for good project management or careful planning.

Myth #4: You need large teams for successful software development

In some cases, adding people to software work can be counterproductive. Software development is a craft and if the wrong people are added to a team, the end result can be very disappointing. I've often been struck by this in big team environments. Getting the numbers right is a tricky job and less is often more. Small teams can often outperform large teams and produce a better end result.

In recent years, there has been much coverage of IT meltdowns in the financial services sector. This is a sector distinguished by highly-staffed projects. I once heard about a Java project in a London bank that had 24 non-coding architects. Most companies will have one architect, possibly even shared across multiple projects. One project with 24 architects seems a little excessive, unless it's a moon landing! It is noteworthy that even with such massive teams, the resulting code may not be so good.

Myth #5: Design is an old-fashioned practice

Bad or no design is simply a case of a wasted opportunity. The resulting code is likely to be disappointing. Design allows for clever elements to be added to software and usually at only modest cost. Adding or fixing design features late in the development cycle can be very expensive. The notion that software design is unnecessary is increasingly pervasive.

Myth #6: Complicated code is a good thing

In an era of mixed programming languages, complicated code is decidedly not a good thing. Downstream maintenance is made much more difficult by the use of needlessly complex code. There is never a good enough reason for producing excessively complex code. At the very least, if it really can't be avoided, such code should be clearly documented to assist the maintainers. Bad code always comes back to haunt some poor soul - someone always has to pay.

Five Steps to Better Coding

What are my five steps to better coding? This is the set of skills that enables a programmer to do the following in a multi-language environment:

1. Read any code, not just your own code
2. Understand any code, not just your own code
3. Safely modify any code, not just your own code
4. Test any code, not just your own code
5. Verify any changed code, not just your own code

I think a comprehensive ability to do the above is closely related to a very well-orchestrated development environment and process. However, in the absence of a such an underlying process, the metrics-based approach provides a good foundation for acquiring the above skills.

For example, when reading code written by another programmer, it is entirely possible that the original programmer has left the organization. In such a case, it is usually up to the newcomer to come to terms with the legacy code. On the other hand, a good team environment can go a long way to helping each member get up to speed. For this reason, it is usually important that the development environment allows for chats. It's amazing how much information can be gleaned from regular short team meetings! In many cases, meetings such as this can help to educate and inform on existing technologies in the organization, development approach, and so on. This information can help newcomers get up to speed and also to ensure good practices are followed. For some reason, many organizations deem such meetings to be a waste of time.

Safe modification and subsequent testing of code is another area where a good sense of support and cooperation is crucial. The same is true of change verification.

All of these skills will be demonstrated in the code examples in the subsequent chapters.

Chapter 1 - Introducing Code Quality Metrics

The Ability to Read Code

Every line of code you write is immediately obsolete. Well, that's perhaps a little extreme. But, it's important to remember that code tends to stick around for a long time to come. So, when you write code it's a good idea to remember that someone else may be tasked with modifying it in the future. How often have you puzzled over some old code, asking yourself what on earth the original programmer was trying to achieve? Don't be the programmer who produces unnecessarily complex or plain bad code.

For this reason, and the fact that most programmers must now code in multiple languages, the ability to read other peoples' code is an extremely important skill. I'll be emphasizing this skill many times in this and later chapters.

Have a look at this article for an example of issues surrounding the protection of legacy code investment: **Protect C++ Legacy Programs by Using Python.**

Code Quality Metrics

I introduce code quality metrics early in the book. The sense in which I use metrics is what might be called macro-quality indicators. In other words, each metric serves as a block quality indicator for a given piece of code. The use of metrics will become second-nature as you progress through the examples in the book.

To get started, here is the first list of metrics I'll use. We'll be applying these metrics as we look more deeply at the associated coding and design issues. The metric-driven approach to coding pretty much applies to most if not all programming languages and I'll illustrate this with multi-language examples.

Reviewing the Code Examples

In an effort to engage my reader, let's assume that you've been tasked with reviewing and fixing the code examples. This will allow for a useful comparison between the metrics approach and your own ideas. It doesn't matter so much if the example uses a language with which you are unfamiliar. I think it's good practice to try to understand multiple languages and I hope the worked examples will help you do this.

Of course, in the real world, it's not always possible to change code. This is particularly so on production systems or systems that have been in service for a long time. On such systems, there may well be a mix of good and bad code. For the purposes of the book, let's assume that the code examples are produced during development and that it is feasible to make improvements.

Let's now have a look at the metrics I'll be using throughout the book.

First Draft Code Quality Metrics - 11 Steps to Better Code

We want to avoid the following in our coding efforts:

- Variable names that are too short and provide no usage context
- Code that provides no context or obvious purpose
- Inconsistent spacing
- Inconsistent parameter type definition
- Incomprehensible code
- Code that is too long
- No exception handling
- No automatic resource management
- External calls that are not contained in separate methods
- Inadequate abstraction - need for higher level code
- Code that is difficult or impossible to change

These metrics represent the rules by which we will judge the quality of the code examples.

Abstraction

I think the metrics are mostly self-explanatory, except perhaps for this one:

- Inadequate abstraction - need for higher level code

I typically use the term abstraction in three contexts. Firstly, abstraction relates to how general a piece of code is. Usually, the more general code is, the more it can be reused. Library code typically is very general. The second sense in which I use the term abstraction relates to code duplication. If code is duplicated, then there is usually scope to abstract (or extract) that code into a function or method. The third sense in which I use abstraction relates to moving substantial items of code into a higher level design pattern, such as a memory block allocator. We'll see examples of all of this as we move through the book.

Abstraction is a powerful concept because it typically sits between the two interdependent procedures of coding and design.

Using the Metrics

So, how do we use these metrics? Well, the metrics are just rules for measuring code quality. Therefore, we need some code to apply them to. So, let's get started with a simple C example to illustrate the metrics in action. Don't worry if you're not familiar with any or all of the languages we'll be looking at. The principles of quality metrics should apply equally to most programming languages. Also, one of the principal aims of the book is to help you learn to read code and this applies to languages with which you have experience as well as languages with which you are unfamiliar.

Being able to get up to speed with a new language is hugely useful in the modern era. This is because new languages and technologies are popping up all over the place. What I hope you'll find after reading this book, is that it is entirely feasible to learn a new language just by following some commonsense practices and applying your experience from other languages.

To get warmed up, what do you think is wrong with the
C code in Listing 1?

Listing 1 - Memory allocation in C code
```
char* a=(char*)malloc(MEMORY_BLOCK_SIZE);
memset(a, 'a', MEMORY_BLOCK_SIZE);
char *b = (char*)malloc(MEMORY_BLOCK_SIZE);
memset(b, 'b', MEMORY_BLOCK_SIZE);
char* c = (char*)malloc(MEMORY_BLOCK_SIZE);
memset(c, 'c', MEMORY_BLOCK_SIZE);
```

The code in Listing 1 allocates and sets the contents of
three blocks of memory. Let's apply the metrics.

Applying Metrics 1-3

1. Variable names that are too short and provide no usage
   context
2. Code that provides no context or obvious purpose
3. Inconsistent spacing

Referring to metrics 1-3, you can see that all of the
variable names in Listing 1 are way too short. At one
character each, the variable names provide no context at
all for divining their purpose. If we assume for learning
purposes that the first variable is in fact a file buffer,
then instead of using `char* a`, would it not be better to
use something like `char* fileBuffer`? At least
then, we have an idea of the purpose of the variable.

Looking at this code in Listing 1, there is really no way
to determine its purpose in the wider codebase in which
it resides. Why do we need the three memory
allocations? Why the calls to `memset`? Would `calloc`
not be a better choice? I'm not saying the code is right or
wrong. It's just hard to determine much about the code
by reading it. When it's hard to read code, it's usually
very hard to change it.

Now, I know an experienced C or C++ programmer will look at Listing 1 and say that it's obvious what the code does: It allocates a few blocks of memory and sets the contents of those blocks. This is absolutely true, but it's not so clear what those memory blocks are used for. Also, when does this memory get de-allocated? Is it leaking memory? I can't easily answer these questions by looking at the code in Listing 1.

The C code in Listing 1 also illustrates inconsistent spacing, i.e., `char* a=(char*)b` and `char *b = (char*)`. Spacing helps in reading code and it's often an important part of adhering to a house style.

Applying Metrics 4-6

- Inconsistent parameter type definition
- Incomprehensible code
- Code that is too long

In Listing 1, we also see inconsistent parameter type definition, i.e., `char* a=(char*)` and `char *b = (char*)`. While not being too serious, this causes the code to be less readable and it may again violate house style guidelines. My personal preference is to use the second version, i.e., `char *b = (char*)` where b is clearly a pointer type.

Comprehensibility reflects how easy is it to determine the programmer's intentions. In Listing 1, the comprehensibility is okay because the code is so simple. But, imagine a few hundred (or many thousands of) lines like those in Listing 1 and maybe then the comprehensibility starts to deteriorate.

Regarding metric 6, Listing 1 is okay. The code can hardly be said to be too long. However, one possible additional defect with Listing 1 is that the calls to `malloc` and `memset` are repeated. As we'll see later on, it might be better to handle this as part of a block allocator design pattern. Code that repeats unnecessarily is often too long. Also, repetition provides fertile ground for programming errors. So, to reduce the repetition, there is probably scope for using a function call.

Applying Metrics 7-9

- No exception handling
- No automatic resource management
- External calls that are not contained in separate methods

What happens in this code if any of the calls to `malloc` fail, e.g., if the host system runs low on memory? That is, where is the exception handling management strategy? For example, if the last `malloc` fails, then the memset following it will write into a random area of memory. And, I do mean random - C code is very lenient in this regard and allows a rogue program to trample all over the host system memory. Not a good problem to encounter late on a Friday and very hard to find and fix in a real-world scenario.

As per metric 8, no automatic resource management is provided in this code. In other words, it is up to the programmer to remember to de-allocate the memory. If the de-allocation is overlooked, then we may get memory leakage. Do this enough times and the system will run out of memory. This is another type of error which is really hard to find and fix.

Closely related to metric 8, external calls (metric 9) are not contained in separate methods (or functions). This is a metric we'll return to because it's so important. For the moment, I simply note in passing that Listing 1 makes direct external calls to `malloc` and `memset`. It is often better practice to provide an external function or method for this type of system service. This latter approach places all calls to `malloc`, `memset`, etc. in a single place. This in turn allows for safer code that centralizes error handling and memory deallocation. We'll see this in action a little later and in the course of the book. This technique is in fact a standard design pattern called **separation of concerns** and helps in dividing up the major tasks in your code.

In this particular case, the resources reserved are in the form of allocated heap memory blocks. This memory will have to be safely returned to the system and this is where a block allocator and block de-allocator pattern will help and we'll see an example of this a little later.

Applying Metrics 10-11

- Inadequate abstraction - need for higher level code
- Code that is difficult or impossible to change

Regarding adequate abstraction, Listing 1 potentially falls down because of the way in which it focuses exclusively on reservation of system resources. The code doesn't seem to fulfil any business requirements. Instead, the memory allocations sit on their own, potentially mixed in with other code (not shown) that does implement business requirements. While this is similar to the above issues pointed to by metrics 8 and 9, the code has a potential lack of abstraction.

For the last metric (number 11), is this code hard to change? Listing 1 uses direct calls to manipulate system memory. If this approach is used throughout the code, rather than using a block allocator, then this can become very hard to change.

Listing 1 Provides Lots of Scope For Errors

So, even in a tiny piece of code, there can be scope for many mistakes ranging from stylistic elements to potentially fatal memory/resource leakage. And, that's even before we look at the underlying code logic or the external calling code.

Using a macroscopic metric-driven approach provides the ability to reject code such as Listing 1 before it becomes part of the target system.

Another Language - Similar Problems

Let's try another code example from another popular language. What do you think about this bash script code in Listing 2? Again, if you're not too familiar with bash scripting, don't worry. Bash is used extensively in Unix and Linux to interact with the operating system and administer tasks such as account management, file deletion, software installation, printing, etc. As in the example above, try to follow the code just by using a commonsense approach. This is a key element of learning to read code.

```
Listing 2 - A simple Linux bash script
#!/bin/sh
cat 'testfile.txt' |
while read line ; do
   echo "Line read: $line"
   outputDirectory=${line##* }
```

```
echo "Output directory: $outputDirectory"
  mv $outputDirectory/streamFolder/output/*.log
$outputDirectory/streamFolder/output/archive/ >
/dev/null 2>&1
  mv $outputDirectory/streamFolder/output/*.txt
$outputDirectory/streamFolder/output/archive/ >
/dev/null 2>&1
done
```

A few comments immediately spring to mind about this code:

- It's quite complicated
- No exception management, e.g., what if one or both of the mv calls happens to fail?
- What if the output directories don't exist (or the disk is full) when mv is called?
- Because of the way it has embedded a string literal, Listing 2 also has weak abstraction

> Regarding adequate abstraction, Listing 2 contains a lot of what is often called 'business logic'. The script reads a file and extracts a directory name. Then, a set of files is moved into an archive subdirectory. This is followed by moving another set of files into the archive subdirectory.

> Business logic is a generic term that relates to the manner in which a piece of software solves a business need. Business logic therefore sits at the all-important boundary between the source code the actual business problem which the software exists to solve.

> In Listing 2, the business logic is the procedure in which files are being moved around between directories. This provides fertile ground for disk-related errors. In its present form, Listing 2 is an optimistic piece of script code. However, in the real world, errors happen and such errors will negatively affect the intended flow of execution. The interrupted flow will then produce unexpected results and disappointment.

This all potentially points to a problem of inadequate abstraction, which in turn leads us into the domain of code design. That is, a better solution than the code in Listing 2 might be to re-implement it using a higher level language than Bash. Of course, there may not be an option to select a given language other than Bash. But, the point is that another language may be a far better option.

One such language is Python. Why? Well, Python provides higher level constructs for doing things like file copies, checking existence (of files and directories), exception handling, and general sequencing of the required operations. This improved abstraction also provides better scope for solving the business problem at hand.

This illustrates an important principle in software development: What is difficult in one language can often be very easy in another more appropriate language. So, a flexible programming mindset can result in a more elegant and generally superior solution. This is design and experience at work and illustrates why a good design can result in a vastly superior end product. Remember, coding and design are not the same thing. We'll see more on this topic later.

As we've seen in Listings 1 and 2, there's a lot of scope for getting into difficulties and in both cases it's just a small amount of code! Bear in mind that real world systems have code sizes up to many millions of lines of code. Bad code has a nasty way of growing.

What about this piece of Python script in Listing 3?

Listing 3 - Python code
```
f=open('myfile','r+')
f.write('abcdef012345')
```

Again, even this small piece of Python code has issues. We'll review and resolve the problems in Listing 3 later on.

Or, how about this piece of PHP script in Listing 4?

Listing 4 - PHP code
```php
function display_all_names() {
  $retrieved_items_list = query_names();
  echo "<select name=\"names\" value=''>Select
Name</option>";
  echo "<option value=\"01\"
selected=\"selected\">All</option>";
  for ($i = 0; $i < count($retrieved_items_list); $i++)
{
    $loopValue = $i + 2;
    echo "<option
value=\"$loopValue\">$retrieved_items_list[$i]</option>
";
  }
  echo "</select>";
}
```

The PHP code in Listing 4 looks quite complicated and has no documentation comments. In fact, Listing 4 is a little bit special in the context of this book because it consists of two separate languages residing alongside each other: PHP and HTML. Two languages and all those strange looking embedded characters suggests that it might be nice to make it a bit clearer with some code comments for the hapless reader/maintainer! In fact, the code in Listing 4 is pretty straightforward. But, in its present form, it might be difficult for a PHP novice to get up to speed with it.

What about this piece of Java JPA code in Listing 5?

Listing 5 - Java code
```java
@Embeddable
public class Address {
  @Column(name = "ADDRESS_STREET")
  private String street;
  @Column(name = "ADDRESS_CITY")
  private String city;

  Address() {}
  public Address(String street, String city) {
    this.street = street;
    this.city = city;
```

```
  }
  public String getStreet() {
     return street;
  }
  public void setStreet(String street) {
     this.street = street;
  }
  public String getCity() {
     return city;
  }
  public void setCity(String city) {
     this.city = city;
  }
  @Override
  public String toString() {
     return "Address [street=" + street + ", city=" +
city + "]";
  }
}
```

Listing 5 is actually pretty good code. It contains many hints about its purpose and this is always helpful in a maintenance or downstream development context. In fact, the bulk of the code in Listing 5 was automatically generated using the excellent Eclipse integrated development environment (IDE). Getting a lot of your code generated for you might seem fanciful. However, such code is far less likely to contain egregious blunders. So, if your IDE allows you to generate code then use it!

I would still say that a small comment in Listing 5 might help a code reader. Something like: "ORM value type for address". This might seem a little cryptic, but it has the merit of giving a reader something to search against, e.g., "ORM". Such hints are very useful when trying to understand someone else's code.

It's possible that Listing 5 looks difficult for readers not conversant with Java object relational mapping (ORM). In short, Listing 5 provides a mapping between a Java class called `Address` and an underlying relational database table. This is actually pretty profound because it indicates how two mainstream technologies live together! In this context, Listing 5 is a true multi-language piece of code.

Notice in Listing 5 the line `@Column(name = "ADDRESS_STREET")`. This is an example of a Java annotation, which describes a column in an external database table. This sounds terribly complicated, but it isn't. Once you define the data members in this class, the rest of the code can be automatically generated. So, to produce something like that in Listing 5, your task is to simply write something like the following Java class code:

```java
public class Address {
  @Column(name = "ADDRESS_STREET")
  private String street;
  @Column(name = "ADDRESS_CITY")
  private String city;
}
```

Then, you can use the code generation tools in Eclipse to create the rest of the code in Listing 5. The generated code is error-free. Modern IDEs such as Eclipse, or IntelliJ IDEA, or NetBeans provide numerous such tools and plugins to make coding easier. This includes tools for automatic code generation, refactoring, method extraction, and so on. Such tools are the programmer's best friend!

For more on getting started with Java ORM, have a look at my article **End-to-End JPA Collections with MySQL, Part 1**

.

Beware of free code

There's a lot of source code available on Internet forums. Much of this code exists to illustrate how to solve certain problems or how to use specific language features. Sometimes, the quality of forum sample code is excellent, other times it can be downright dangerous. Have a look at a typical sample of bad code in Listing 6 and see what you think of it.

Listing 6 - Some forum C code

```c
include<fftw3.h>

int main(void)
{
   int N;
   fftw_complex *in, *out;
   fftw_plan my_plan;
   in = (fftw_complex*)
fftw_malloc(sizeof(fftw_complex)*N);
   out = (fftw_complex*)
fftw_malloc(sizeof(fftw_complex)*N);
   /* Populate the in array with data */
   my_plan = fftw_plan_dft_1d(N, in, out, FFTW_FORWARD,
FFTW_ESTIMATE);
   fftw_execute(my_plan);

   return 0;
}
```

On the face of it, the code in Listing 6 looks pretty okay. It uses a library called FFTW. However, notice the calls to `fftw_malloc`. These calls allocate memory and there is no corresponding call to `fftw_free`. The result is that this code leaks memory. Now, in such a simple piece of code, the memory will be reclaimed once the `return` from main occurs (i.e., when the program exits). But, if the Listing 6 code was contained inside a function or inside a library, then the concomitant memory leakage could have serious implications.

We saw the issue of memory leakage earlier in Listing 1 with undisciplined calls to `malloc`. This is similar in that the reserved resources are not being returned to the system.

I recall a situation when a programmer was writing C memory allocation functions with code similar to that in Listing 6. As the code ran for a longish period, memory leaks started to reduce the amount of free memory in the host system. Pretty soon, the system was brought to its knees. The initial suggestion was to reboot the host machine (it was a long time ago!). After a time, this was seen to be an unworkable fix.

The next 'solution' was to upgrade the memory in the host system. This solution of course just provided a temporary reprieve and the increasingly beleaguered programmer was soon back to square one with code that continued to leak memory like a sieve.

The end result was a pretty disastrous product that was beset by problems from day one and was eventually retired long before it reached the end of its lifecycle. It's generally easier, cheaper, and a lot less disappointing to get the code right to start with.

Let's have a look at another typical piece of forum code in Listing 7 and see if it meets the demands of our metric-driven approach. This C code opens a file - what could be simpler?

Listing 7 - Some more forum C code
```
FILE *fp;
fp=fopen("c:\\ATestFile.txt", "w");
fprintf(fp, "Testing...\n");
```

Here come the metrics and a brief assessment of the Listing 7 code.

1. Variable names that are too short and provide no usage context
2. Code that provides no context or obvious purpose

3. Inconsistent spacing
4. Inconsistent parameter type definition
5. Incomprehensible code
6. Code that is too long
7. No exception handling
8. No automatic resource management
9. External calls that are not contained in separate methods
10. Inadequate abstraction - need for higher level code
11. Code that is difficult or impossible to change

The variable name `fp` might be said to be too short (metric 1). There is also inconsistent spacing (metric 3) in the line

```
fp=fopen("c:\\ATestFile.txt","w");,
```

which might be improved as `fp =`

```
fopen("c:\\ATestFile.txt", "w");`.
```
There is no exception handling (metric 7) in Listing 7 - what happens if the call to `fopen` fails? There is no automatic resource management (metric 8), i.e., the allocated file doesn't get closed. So, we may have resource leakage. External calls (such as `fopen`)are not contained in separate resource allocation methods (metric 9).

That's a lot of issues in just 3 lines of code.

The use of metrics allows us to diagnose pretty much any code in pretty much any mainstream language. Without even running the code, you can see the major issues and objections. This is a powerful approach and allows for a useful degree of early checking. This is important because it's worth remembering that a runtime system may in fact be quite forgiving of low-quality code, but in the long run bad code will always come back to haunt the originator or the maintainer.

In chapter 2, we'll look at some techniques for helping to fix and avoid some of the problems we've seen so far in the code examples.

Chapter Summary

Coding is not easy. Metrics allow for a set of useful rules to be applied to the code even before running it. This in turn can help you avoid a lot of problems early on in the development cycle. Applying metrics in this way can substantially improve the code quality. Another nice thing about metrics is that they can be augmented as required. If another metric makes sense, then you can just add it to the existing set.

Very often, the same problems are seen in different programming languages, e.g., non-existent or poor exception management, inadequate abstraction, weak design, excessive complexity, and so on. Indeed, one might say that it is all too easy to produce poor quality code in any language. Nonetheless, metrics can help in fixing and avoiding these problems.

In addition to the use of metrics, machine-generated code can provide another big boost to programmer productivity. Indeed, modern IDEs such as Eclipse facilitate programming quality with tools for code generation, refactoring, exception coding, etc. Such tools are the programmer's best friend.

Beware of forum code. Remember that free code should be carefully reviewed before use. Very often, forum code is simply a very rough guideline rather than being complete production-grade code.

Chapter 2 - Using Code Quality Metrics To Refactor C

Having identified our initial set of metrics in the previous chapter, let's now put them to work. I'll rework one of the chapter 1 C code examples using the metrics as a kind of guiding hand. Of necessity, this procedure crosses over from pure coding into the domain of software design. I think this is a good thing. Moving easily between design and coding is a key skill in effective programming. Also, remember that IDEs such as, Eclipse and NetBeans have excellent facilities for code refactoring. This includes: method extraction, constant definition, interface definition, and so on. Any investment in learning to use these tools will pay you dividends for years in the form of more robust code.

So, without further ado, let's now use the C code from Chapter 1, Listing 1 and refactor it following the metric analysis. For easy reference, here's the original code.

```c
int main() {
  char* a=(char*)malloc(MEMORY_BLOCK_SIZE);
  memset(a, 'a', MEMORY_BLOCK_SIZE);
  char *b = (char*)malloc(MEMORY_BLOCK_SIZE);
  memset(b, 'b', MEMORY_BLOCK_SIZE);
  char* c = (char*)malloc(MEMORY_BLOCK_SIZE);
  memset(c, 'c', MEMORY_BLOCK_SIZE);
  return 0;
}
```

The first effort at a reworked version of the code is illustrated in Listing 1. I've tried to fix some of the metric-related problems we saw in Chapter 1 - namely: variable naming, spacing, inconsistent parameter type definition, and exception/error handling.

Listing 1 - Reworked post-metric C code

```
int main() {
  char *blockA = (char*)malloc(MEMORY_BLOCK_SIZE);
  if (blockA) {
    memset(blockA, 'a', MEMORY_BLOCK_SIZE);
  }
  char *blockB = (char*)malloc(MEMORY_BLOCK_SIZE);
  if (blockB) {
    memset(blockB, 'b', MEMORY_BLOCK_SIZE);
  }
  char *blockC = (char*)malloc(MEMORY_BLOCK_SIZE);
  if (blockC) {
    memset(blockC, 'c', MEMORY_BLOCK_SIZE);
  }
  return 0;
}
```

In the spirit of metric-driven iteration, let's refer again to the metrics on the modified code and see how it stacks up.

1) Variable names that are too short and provide no usage context - **better now** (parameter a is now blockA, b is now blockB, and c is now blockC)
2) Code that provides no context or obvious purpose - **not much better now**
3) Inconsistent spacing - **better now** (notice the use of spaces to improve readability)
4) Inconsistent parameter type definition - **better now** (the pointers all use the same format of: char *blockA)
5) Incomprehensible code - **not much better now**
6) Code that is too long - **not much better now**
7) No exception handling - **better now** (I now check that the calls to malloc succeeded)
8) No automatic resource management - **not much better now**
9) External calls that are not contained in separate methods - **not much better now**
10) Inadequate abstraction - need for higher level code - **not much better now**
11) Code that is difficult or impossible to change - **not much better now**

According to four of the metrics, we've made some progress with the code. But, there's still scope for improvement. So, let's make some more changes to try to more fully satisfy the metrics. In particular, in Listing 2, I introduce a block allocator function to take care of the memory allocations and thereby improve the resource management and the level of abstraction, i.e., metrics 8 to 11.

Listing 2 - Second attempt at reworked post-metric C code (adding a block allocator)

```
char* blockAllocator(int blockSize)
  /* Pass in a required block size and attempt to
allocate the memory. If
  allocation fails, log it and return NULL.*/
{
  char* blockAllocated = (char*)malloc(blockSize);
  if (blockAllocated) {
    return blockAllocated;
  } else {
    /* Log the memory allocation error */
    return NULL;
  }
}

int main() {
  /* Allocate 3 memory blocks for use in caching */
  char* blockA = blockAllocator(MEMORY_BLOCK_SIZE);
  if (blockA) {
    memset(blockA, 'a', MEMORY_BLOCK_SIZE);
  }
  char* blockB = blockAllocator(MEMORY_BLOCK_SIZE);
  if (blockB) {
    memset(blockB, 'b', MEMORY_BLOCK_SIZE);
  }
  char* blockC = blockAllocator(MEMORY_BLOCK_SIZE);
  if (blockC) {
    memset(blockC, 'c', MEMORY_BLOCK_SIZE);
  }
  return 0;
}
```

After this change, let's now see how the metrics stack up.

- Variable names that are too short and provide no usage context - **better now**
- Code that provides no context or obvious purpose - **better now**
- Inconsistent spacing - **better now**
- Inconsistent parameter type definition - **better now**
- Incomprehensible code - **better now**
- Code that is too long - **better now**
- No exception handling - **better now**
- No automatic resource management - **a bit better now**
- External calls that are not contained in separate methods - **better now**
- Inadequate abstraction - need for higher level code - **better now**
- Code that is difficult or impossible to change - **better now**

The code has improved now that the resource allocations happen in a separate function. In fact, the addition of a block allocator has incorporated nearly all of the metrics. The main code is easier to understand now that resource allocation has been separated into its own function. This has also helped make the code more specific to solving the business problem, rather than handling memory allocation issues. This is what I mean by improving the abstraction level. Also, the code is now more changeable because of the improved separation of concerns.

However, there is still scope for improvement, e.g., we should also add a block de-allocator function. This would then take care of returning the allocated memory to the free pool. Here's a simple example of adding such a block de-allocator function in Listing 3.

```
Listing 3 - Third attempt at reworked post-metric C
code (adding a
block deallocator)
char* blockAllocator(int blockSize)
```

```
  /* Pass in a required block size and attempt to
allocate the memory. If
  allocation fails, log it and return NULL.*/
{
  char* blockAllocated = (char*)malloc(blockSize);
  if (blockAllocated) {
    return blockAllocated;
  } else {
    /* Log the memory allocation error */
    return NULL;
  }
}

int blockDeAllocator(char* memoryBlock)
  /* Pass in a block to de-allocate and attempt to de-
allocate it. If
  de-allocation fails, log it and return -1, otherwise
return 0.*/
{
  if(memoryBlock) {
    free(memoryBlock);
  } else {
    /* Log the memory attempt to de-allocate a NULL
block */
    return -1;
  }
  return 0;
}

int main() {
  /* Allocate memory blocks for use in caching */
  char* blockA = blockAllocator(MEMORY_BLOCK_SIZE);
  if (blockA) {
    memset(blockA, 'a', MEMORY_BLOCK_SIZE);
  }
  char* blockB = blockAllocator(MEMORY_BLOCK_SIZE);
  if (blockB) {
    memset(blockB, 'b', MEMORY_BLOCK_SIZE);
  }
  char* blockC = blockAllocator(MEMORY_BLOCK_SIZE);
  if (blockC) {
    memset(blockC, 'c', MEMORY_BLOCK_SIZE);
  }

  // Lots more code in here

  blockDeAllocator(blockA);
```

```
  blockDeAllocator(blockB);
  blockDeAllocator(blockC);

  return 0;
}
```

What do you think is missing in the calls to
blockDeAllocator in main?

How about a check on the return code? This would be a
good idea in order to make certain that the de-allocation
occurred as planned. One other thing to add would be to
set the block pointers to NULL. This ensures that the
pointers are returned to a known state. With this last set
of changes, the finished code looks like that in Listing 4.

Listing 4 - The final iteration of the reworked post-metric
C code (checking the deallocator result)
```
char* blockAllocator(int blockSize)
  /* Pass in a required block size and attempt to
allocate the memory. If
  allocation fails, log it and return NULL.*/
{
  char* blockAllocated = (char*)malloc(blockSize);
  if (blockAllocated) {
    return blockAllocated;
  } else {
    /* Log the memory allocation error */
    return NULL;
  }
}

int blockDeAllocator(char* memoryBlock)
  /* Pass in a block to de-allocate and attempt to de-
allocate it. If
  de-allocation fails, log it and return -1, otherwise
return 0.*/
{
  if(memoryBlock) {
    free(memoryBlock);
  } else {
    /* Log the memory attempt to de-allocate a NULL
block */
    return -1;
```

```
    }
    return 0;
  }

int main() {
  /* Allocate memory blocks for use in caching */
  char* blockA = blockAllocator(MEMORY_BLOCK_SIZE);
  if (blockA) {
    memset(blockA, 'a', MEMORY_BLOCK_SIZE);
  }
  char* blockB = blockAllocator(MEMORY_BLOCK_SIZE);
  if (blockB) {
    memset(blockB, 'b', MEMORY_BLOCK_SIZE);
  }
  char* blockC = blockAllocator(MEMORY_BLOCK_SIZE);
  if (blockC) {
    memset(blockC, 'c', MEMORY_BLOCK_SIZE);
  }

  // Lots more code here

  if (blockDeAllocator(blockA) != 0) {
    cout << "We got an error with blockA" << endl;
  } else {
    cout << "No error with blockA" << endl;
  }
  if (blockDeAllocator(blockB) != 0) {
    cout << "We got an error with blockB" << endl;
  } else {
    cout << "No error with blockB" << endl;
  }
  if (blockDeAllocator(blockC) != 0) {
    cout << "We got an error with blockC" << endl;
  } else {
    cout << "No error with blockC" << endl;
  }
  return 0;
}
```

Now, clearly the code in Listing 4 is still not finished!
We really should also add a logging function to the
blockAllocator and blockDeAllocator
functions. This would typically write the results to disk
of all allocation and de-allocation operations. Also, we
could invoke memset inside the allocator function.

The important point to note is that once the code has been modularized, it can then be further improved. The use of metrics helps to produce a more robust solution and in a nice iterative fashion.

All this probably seems like a lot of work. What do we gain from this exercise in metrics consultation and refactoring? Well, for one thing we can now accurately track all memory resource allocations and de-allocations. This might not seem to be a big deal on a powerful developer workstation or a large production server. But, memory scarcity is often a fact of life on on modern embedded platforms (such as phones or tablets). Such devices can run short of memory and at least now you have the potential for extracting some details if problems occur. Memory leaks should always be fixed.

In effect, you have designed much stronger code as a result of the use of the simple metric set introduced in Chapter 1. Remember the 4 S's? This is coding for:

1. Safety
2. Security
3. Simplicity
4. Survivability

The code in Listing 4 is a lot closer to implementing the above 4 S's than its more primitive counterpart in Listing 1.

Code reuse

There is a further merit of the separate `blockAllocator` and `blockDeAllocator` functions from Listing 4. This is that these two functions can become potential candidates for inclusion in an external library. In this way, code written in one project can be generalised and carried into other future projects.

So, the use of the metrics provides a nice iterative model for coding. You draw up a simple design, write some code, consult the metrics, and make some incremental changes. Then consult the metrics again, make some changes as required, and so on, repeating the cycle until you are satisfied with the results. Clearly, this should all be done as you carefully test the code.

I should point out that this is not a revolutionary procedure! Good programmers work this way all the time. However, there is a lot of code out there that is not produced in a metric-driven fashion.

Chapter Summary

A metrics-based approach to refactoring C is both iterative and straightforward. The example C code I used is pretty simple, but it clearly illustrates the required principles. The code produced by following the metrics is easier to read and more reliable with far better separation of concerns. Such code is easier to understand and maintain.

Metrics-driven refactoring helps to produce more general code. This is invariably a good thing because more general code is usually more reusable. Such code can be used in multiple projects and is often a candidate for inclusion in a library. Aside from libraries, code that is written in a more general way facilitates the creation of frameworks. Such frameworks can become powerful productivity tools.

Code problem diagnosis becomes a lot easier using metrics. Obviously, as a programmer becomes more experienced, the metrics become second-nature.

Chapter 3 - Using Code Quality Metrics To Refactor Bash and Python Code

Having now seen metrics-driven refactoring applied to C code, let's now see how it does with other languages: namely Bash and Python.

In Chapter 1, Listing 2, we saw the following Bash code.

```sh
#!/bin/sh
cat 'testfile.txt' |
while read line ; do
  echo "Line read: $line"
  outputDirectory=${line##* }
  echo "Output directory: $outputDirectory"
  mv $outputDirectory/streamFolder/output/*.log
$outputDirectory/streamFolder/output/archive/ >
/dev/null 2>&1
  mv $outputDirectory/streamFolder/output/*.txt
$outputDirectory/streamFolder/output/archive/ >
/dev/null 2>&1
done
```

Let's now apply the coding metrics to the above Bash script. Again, here is the list of metrics.

1. Variable names that are too short and provide no usage context
2. Code that provides no context or obvious purpose
3. Inconsistent spacing
4. Inconsistent parameter type definition
5. Incomprehensible code
6. Code that is too long
7. No exception handling
8. No automatic resource management
9. External calls that are not contained in separate methods

10. Inadequate abstraction - need for higher level code
11. Code that is difficult or impossible to change

Out of the metrics, I think only a few apply in the case of this Bash code. This is an important issue: In real world code, don't expect it to be all bad! If you're modifying legacy code, the original author may well have done a great job with it. If this is the case, then your task is easier.

In this case, the required change may be straightforward. However, there may also arise a case where you can make an improvement as part of another change. We'll see this in the present example.

So, in my opinion the Bash code violates metrics 7 and 10 only:

- No exception handling
- Inadequate abstraction - need for higher level code

Why is this the case? Well, the calls to mv can fail and we won't know about it. This is because the script is coded to swallow output and errors. How do I know this? The clue is in the redirect code: `> /dev/null 2>&1`. This has the intentional effect of not letting us see the result of the preceding mv operation.

So, as per metric 7, we need to at least record if an exception occurs in the calls to mv.

In regard to inadequate abstraction, the file name can be made into a constant. Then, the constant can be referenced in the script. This is better than embedding the name as a literal string value, particularly if the file name is used in multiple places in the script. A downstream maintainer might be tasked with changing the script and could easily forget to change the file name in all places. Defining the file name as a constant avoids this unpleasant possibility.

So, with all of the above observations in mind, Listing 1 is the modified version of the Bash code.

Listing 1 Post-metric Bash code

```sh
#!/bin/sh
readonly fileName='testfile.txt'

cat $fileName |
while read line ; do
  echo "Line read: $line"
  outputDirectory=${line##* }
  echo "Output directory: $outputDirectory"
  mv $outputDirectory/streamFolder/output/*.log
$outputDirectory/streamFolder/output/archive/ >
/dev/null 2>&1
  error=$?
  if [ $error -ne 0 ] ; then
    echo "First mv failed with exit code of $error"
  fi
  mv $outputDirectory/streamFolder/output/*.txt
$outputDirectory/streamFolder/output/archive/ >
/dev/null 2>&1
  error=$?
  if [ $error -ne 0 ] ; then
    echo "Second mv failed with exit code of $error"
  fi
done
```

Notice in Listing 1 that we now have a constant called fileName representing the file name. This constant can now be used throughout the script instead of embedding the file name. So, if a different file name is required at some future time, then it has to be changed in just one place instead of potentially multiple places in the script.

The other major change is to store and examine the error code from each of the mv calls. This allows us to know for sure if the mv call succeeded or not. To complete the example, it would probably make sense to log the error code details to disk. But, you get the idea! Following the metrics helps to take the guesswork out of the code, particularly when errors occur.

There is still an issue with inadequate abstraction (metric 10) in Listing 1. Can you see it? The new error handling code is an improvement, but it has introduced a problem with code duplication. We should really try to fix this, and one way to do this is to abstract the error handling code itself into a function. Listing 2 illustrates the final offering for the Bash code.

Listing 2 Second iteration of the post-metric Bash code

```sh
#!/bin/sh

readonly fileName='testfile.txt'

errorHandler() {
  echo $1
  echo $2
  if [ $2 -ne 0 ] ; then
    echo "Failed in errorHandler $1 Exit code is $2"
  fi
}

cat $fileName |
while read line ; do
  echo "Line read: $line"
  outputDirectory=${line##* }
  echo "Output directory: $outputDirectory"
  mv $outputDirectory/streamFolder/output/*.log
$outputDirectory/streamFolder/output/archive/ >
/dev/null 2>&1
  errorHandler "first call to mv", $?
  mv $outputDirectory/streamFolder/output/*.txt
$outputDirectory/streamFolder/output/archive/ >
/dev/null 2>&1
  errorHandler "second call to mv", $?
done
```

Now, any failures that occur during execution of the code in Listing 2 appear as illustrated in Listing 3. These errors can be logged to disk if required by adding more code to the errorHandler function.

Listing 3 - Running the modified Bash code

```
Line read: mydirectory
Output directory: mydirectory
```

```
first call to mv,
1
Failed in errorHandler first call to mv, Exit code is 1
second call to mv,
1
Failed in errorHandler second call to mv, Exit code is
1
```

Notice also, that by following the metrics the script in Listing 2 is nicely divided (or modularized) into three parts:

- Definition of constants
- Definition of error handler and other functions
- The main code

Also noteworthy in this example was the fact that we iterated twice through the metrics. Again, this is a good practice - making small, focused changes, reviewing the changes, and adding more small changes. The combination of the small changes adds up to a far better end result and the code can be tested carefully as you go.

One noteworthy caveat is in relation to spacing. There might be a temptation on the part of a Java (or other high level language) programmer to introduce spaces into Listing 2. This might be done to try to improve readability. One of the things about scripting languages, such as, Bash and Python is that they are often very fussy about spaces, indentation, and so on. Adding spaces to Bash code can introduce hard to find errors. So, be careful with readability requirements!

Up to this point, we've seen the metrics in action in C code and now in Bash scripting. How can the metrics approach be applied to Python code? Let's find out.

A Python example

In Chapter 1, Listing 3, we saw the following Python code.

```python
f=open('myfile','r+')
f.write('abcdef012345')
```

As usual, let's apply the metrics to the Python code. Again, here is the list of metrics.

1. Variable names that are too short and provide no usage context
2. Code that provides no context or obvious purpose
3. Inconsistent spacing
4. Inconsistent parameter type definition
5. Incomprehensible code
6. Code that is too long
7. No exception handling
8. No automatic resource management
9. External calls that are not contained in separate methods
10. Inadequate abstraction - need for higher level code
11. Code that is difficult or impossible to change

I would say that the following metrics are violated by the Python code:

- Variable names that are too short and provide no usage context
- Inconsistent spacing
- No exception handling
- No automatic resource management
- External calls that are not contained in separate methods

Also, we have some assumptions lying at the heart of the Python code example.

What are the assumptions? Well, the first line assumes that the file already exists and the second line in turn assumes that the first line was successful. In other words, an exception is thrown if the file does not exist.

A simpler and sturdier version is illustrated in Listing 4 where we use the standard exception management of the Python language. Also, I've tried to improve the file handle name by giving it some context in the wider program.

Listing 4 - Incorporating better naming and exception management

```
try:
   logfile = open('myfile', 'r+')
   logfile.write('abcdef012345')
except IOError:
   print('Encountered an error')
```

Now if the file is deleted before the script runs, then you get a meaningful message rather than a runtime failure. It's important to always remember that when your code interacts with system resources (such as files), you're handling somebody else's property! System resources are owned by the system, so you have to handle them with care.

The moral of the story is: Keep it simple and try to avoid assumptions. Mother nature enjoys assumptions; they give her an opportunity to show us who's boss!

The addition of exception code has still not produced particularly reliable operation. We are still relying on the file existing in order for the code to work. To fix this, before opening the file, we can first check that it exists as illustrated in Listing 5:

Listing 5 - Incorporating an existence check

```
try:
   if(os.path.isfile('myfile')):
     logfile = open('myfile', 'r+')
     logfile.write('abcdef012345')
   else:
     print('File does not exist')
except IOError:
   print('Encountered an error')
```

So, the code now uses `isfile()` to check if the file exists before attempting to open and update it. This means that we have now removed the assumption about the file existence. If the file does not exist, then we'll know upfront, rather than relying on an exception. However, there's still a troublesome problem with this code. Can you see it?

Race condition

While the code has been improved, there exists a potential race condition if someone deletes the file just after the script runs (and passes the existence test). Who says coding is easy! The race condition occurs if the file is deleted unexpectedly, e.g., just before the call to open(). If the race condition occurs, then the code will produce an error something like this:

```
Traceback (most recent call last):
  File "<stdin>", line 1, in <module>
IOError: [Errno 2] No such file or directory: 'myfile'
```

Fixing the race condition is more difficult because it involves administrative policies (e.g., instructions such as: "Do not delete this file"). This is one of the reasons why the extensive use of files for data access may not necessarily be the best design approach. Instead, databases provide a more reliable data repository and this is why suitable database APIs exist for all the mainstream languages.

Remember, if you think a race condition can't occur in your code, it probably will.

What's kind of interesting about this exercise with Chapter 1 Listing 3 is the relative subtlety of the underlying issues. This is just a few lines of code. And, we're not done yet! Remember, once we start to use files in our code, we must then start to think about responsible resource management. This is because the files are the property of the host system.

Resource management and state control

Notice that the file referred to in the Listing 5 code may still be open at the end of the script. Once the script exits, the file will be closed but this is not good citizenship! Any and all allocated resources should always be returned to the system before the script exits. How can we ensure that the script cleans up after itself and the file is closed? This requires another few changes - adding a `finally` clause as illustrated in Listing 6:

Listing 6 - Adding a finally clause and restructuring the code

```
logfile = None
try:
  if(os.path.isfile('myfile')):
    logfile = open('myfile', 'r+')
    logfile.write('abcdef012345')
  else:
    print('File does not exist')
except IOError:
  print('Encountered an error')
finally:
  if(logfile != None):
    if(logfile.closed == False):
      logfile.close()
    else:
      print('File was None')
```

In Listing 6, we now move the file handle definition (and its initialization to the value None) outside of the main loop. This means that the file handle is in scope when we leave the try clause. The finally clause is guaranteed to run and this gives us the means for deallocating the file object based on its state.

The code is still not perfect, but it's a lot more robust now than the original rather laconic and brittle two-line effort:

```
f=open('myfile','r+')
f.write('abcdef012345')
```

The finished code in Listing 6 is longer than the original version, but it is a much better piece of work. One might say that, in this case, more is more!

A slightly more complex multi-language example

Let's now have a look at a slightly more complex example in Listing 7 where we have some Python code that invokes a standalone C++ program.

```
Listing 7 - Python invocation of a C++ program
import os, errno
import subprocess as sp

def invokeProgram():
  try:
    print('Just before Python program invocation')

p=sp.Popen(['/home/CPlusPlus0xProject'],stdout=sp.PIPE)
    result = p.communicate()[0]
    print('CPlusPlus0xProject invoked' + result +
'\n')
  except OSError as e:
    print('Exception handler error occurred: ' +
str(e.errno) + '\n')
```

```
if __name__ == '__main__':
    invokeProgram()
```

So, what's going on in Listing 7?

As before, we now put on our code reader hat and apply some common sense in order to decipher the code in Listing 7. The most complicated thing in Listing 7 is the following:

```
    p = sp.Popen(['/home/CPlusPlus0xProject'], stdout =
sp.PIPE)
```

If you think that the call to `sp.Popen` spawns a new process, you're right! In fact, it invokes a C++ executable program called `CPlusPlus0xProject`. In order to let you see what's happening, program output from `CPlusPlus0xProject` is directed using a pipe to standard output. Now that we have a rough idea of what's going on in Listing 7, let's apply the metrics and see if the code can be improved. Remember, that it is our ongoing brief in the book to try to understand and then improve the code examples using the metrics approach.

Applying the metrics

As usual, here are the metrics:

1. Variable names that are too short and provide no usage context
2. Code that provides no context or obvious purpose
3. Inconsistent spacing
4. Inconsistent parameter type definition
5. Incomprehensible code
6. Code that is too long
7. No exception handling
8. No automatic resource management
9. External calls that are not contained in separate methods
10. Inadequate abstraction - need for higher level code

11. Code that is difficult or impossible to change

I would say that the following metrics are violated by the Python code:

1 Variable names that are too short and provide no usage context
2 Inconsistent spacing
3 No automatic resource management
4 Inadequate abstraction - need for higher level code

Let's try to address these concerns with some focused changes as illustrated in Listing 8.

Listing 8 - Python invocation of a C++ program

```python
import os, errno
import subprocess as sp

def invokeProgram():
  try:
  cProcess = None
  try:
    print('Just before Python program invocation')
    cProcess = sp.Popen(['/home/CPlusPlus0xProject'],
stdout = sp.PIPE)
    result = cProcess.communicate()[0]
    print('CPlusPlus0xProject invoked' + result +
os.linesep)
  except OSError as e:
    print('Exception handler error occurred: ' +
str(e.errno) + os.linesep)
  finally:
    print('Value of cprocess is ' + str(cProcess))
    try:
      if(cProcess != None):
        cProcess.terminate()
    except OSError as e:
      print('Second exception handler error occurred: '
+ str(e.errno) + os.linesep)

if __name__ == '__main__':
    invokeProgram()
```

Instead of using a single-character variable (i.e., p = sp.Popen(['/home/CPlusPlus0xProject'], stdout = sp.PIPE) in Listing 7), I now use the more descriptive name cProcess in Listing 8. This name choice also reflects the fact that we are spawning a C++ program, which provides a hint to the programmer concerning the purpose of the code. Remember, a maintenance programmer may have little idea about the code.

I've also improved the spacing for readability in the line:

```
  cProcess = sp.Popen(['/home/CPlusPlus0xProject'],
stdout = sp.PIPE)
```

Notice also in Listing 8 the way we now terminate the spawned process using cProcess.terminate(). This ensures, once again, that any allocated resources are deleted before the code exits. In order to enforce this policy, I also had to move the declaration of the cProcess to just before the beginning of the try-catch-finally statement.

Lastly, in relation to improving abstraction, I now use the platform-agnostic symbol for a newline, namely: os.linesep. This is good practice because it makes the code more general and not tied to any specific runtime platform.

Chapter Summary

We've seen how metrics can be applied to improve C and C++ code. Metrics can also be applied to both Bash and Python code. Another use case for metrics is where Python code is used to call a high level language program, such as, one written in C++.

Bash script code is quite low level and has a fairly arcane syntax, e.g., you capture an error/return code using the rather forgettable symbol: $?. However, it is interesting to see that a metric-driven approach is very applicable to Bash scripting. Indeed, the end result can be a very well structured script. Such a script becomes easier to understand and to modify if required. One important point to note about refactoring Bash is to watch out for spaces. Don't be too cavalier about introducing spaces into Bash code - the end result can be disappointing!

Python is also a good candidate for using code quality metrics. This is because Python is itself a relatively high-level language, which means that the structural enhancements that come from using metrics can help to make the code easier to read and modify. In addition, by making the code more abstract, it can potentially be made ready to run on a wider range of platforms.

Chapter 4 - Using Code Quality Metrics To Refactor Java

Having now introduced some metrics and illustrated their use in examining and refactoring C, Bash, and Python code, let's now do some more metric exercises, this time using Java as the target language. As we've seen, the metrics procedure simply means selecting some code and examining its contents and determining how it stacks up against those metrics.

The programming area I look at in this chapter is that of handling Java exceptions. Why is this important? Well, code exceptions are a constant fact of programming life. Exceptions can occur when your code tries to open a non-existent file or for any of a huge number of reasons.

Skillful coding of exception handlers is indispensable in modern multi-language development environments. Traditionally, coding has tended to focus initially on producing the core functionality. Only then, is the exception handling added. This is a good approach, but now that multiple languages are in common use, I think it may be better to write the core code around the potential exception producers.

There is literally tons of Java code available in online forums. It's interesting to look at some of the code and see what the quality is like. For the first check, I've selected some code from an article I wrote way back in 2009. The article discusses the use of interceptors inside JBoss applications and the full version is available at - **Nonlinear Code Management in EJB3**. The article concerns some important design issues around loose coupling and cross cutting concerns in the EJB3 environment.

Have a look at the Java code in Listing 1 and see can you spot anything suspicious or potentially risky.

Listing 1 - Some JBoss Java Code

```java
public class ExecutionProfiler
{
  @AroundInvoke
  public Object profile(InvocationContext invocation)
throws Exception
  {
    long startTimeSnapshot=System.currentTimeMillis();

    System.out.println("Now at the beginning of the
interceptor method " +
      invocation.getMethod() + " startTimeSnapshot " +
startTimeSnapshot);

    try
    {
      return invocation.proceed();
    }
    finally
    {
      long endTimeSnapshot=System.currentTimeMillis();
      long executionTime=System.currentTimeMillis()-
startTimeSnapshot;
      System.out.println("Now at the end of the
interceptor method " +
        invocation.getMethod() + " endTimeSnapshot "  +
endTimeSnapshot);
      System.out.println("Method " +
invocation.getMethod()
        + " time taken: " + executionTime + "
milliseconds");
    }
  }
}
```

Let's have a look at the metrics.

Applying the metrics

As usual, let's apply the metrics to the Java code. Again, here is the list of metrics.

1. Variable names that are too short and provide no usage context
2. Code that provides no context or obvious purpose
3. Inconsistent spacing
4. Inconsistent parameter type definition
5. Incomprehensible code
6. Code that is too long
7. No exception handling
8. No automatic resource management
9. External calls that are not contained in separate methods
10. Inadequate abstraction - need for higher level code
11. Code that is difficult or impossible to change

Looking at the code in Listing 1, it's not too bad. The method is called `profile()`, which gives a good solid hint about its purpose. An educated guess would suggest that this code serves to provide some timing details for execution profiling. It turns out this is correct. So, the choice of a meaningful name by the author has helped the downstream user (that's us). The spacing is a little bit off in lines such as: `long startTimeSnapshot=System.currentTimeMillis()`, so we can fix those with ease.

1. Variable names that are too short and provide no usage context - **no change needed**
2. Code that provides no context or obvious purpose - **no change needed**
3. Inconsistent spacing - **better now** (notice the use of spaces in Listing 2, to improve readability)
4. Inconsistent parameter type definition - **no change needed**
5. Incomprehensible code - **no change needed**
6. Code that is too long - **no change needed**
7. No exception handling - **needs attention**
8. No automatic resource management - **no change needed**
9. External calls that are not contained in separate methods - **no change needed**

10. Inadequate abstraction - need for higher level code - **needs attention**
11. Code that is difficult or impossible to change - **no change needed**

Metric 3 Issue Related to Spaces

Listing 2 illustrates improved spacing to facilitate comprehension.

Metric 7 Issue Related to Exception Management

One thing comes to mind in relation to the exception block: Where is the `catch` clause? Is it not possible for this code to throw any type of exception? If this is the case, then the code is fine. However, if the `try` clause throws an exception, then there is no handler for such an exception. What happens in this case? Well, execution is guaranteed to resume in the `finally` clause. The problem with this is that the code might well be unstable at this point, e.g., there might potentially be files or database connections left open. So, I would suggest that an improved version is as illustrated in Listing 2.

Metric 10 Issue Related to Abstraction

The use of `System.out.println` is a bit primitive. It would be better to direct this output to a logging facility, such as, Log4J.

Post-metric Updated Code

Listing 2 illustrates the Java code after examination with the metrics.

Listing 2 - Some Improved JBoss Java Code

```java
public class ExecutionProfiler
{
  @AroundInvoke
  public Object profile(InvocationContext invocation)
throws Exception
  {
    boolean exceptionOccurred = false;
    long startTimeSnapshot =
System.currentTimeMillis();

    System.out.println("Now at the beginning of the
interceptor method " +
      invocation.getMethod() + " startTimeSnapshot " +
startTimeSnapshot);

    try
    {
      return invocation.proceed();
    }
    catch (Exception exc)
    {
      exceptionOccurred = true;
      System.err.println("Exception: " +
exc.getMessage());
      // Do something with the exception, cleanup,
close files, etc.
    }
    finally
    {
      if(!exceptionOccurred) {
        long endTimeSnapshot =
System.currentTimeMillis();
        long executionTime = System.currentTimeMillis()
- startTimeSnapshot;
        System.out.println("Now at the end of the
interceptor method " +
          invocation.getMethod() + " endTimeSnapshot "
+ endTimeSnapshot);
```

```
        System.out.println("Method " +
invocation.getMethod()
            + " time taken: " + executionTime + "
milliseconds");
    }
  }
 }
}
```

Listing 2 is now less brittle than Listing 1 because it takes account of any exceptions that occur. I note in passing that the approach used in Listing 1 is very common, i.e., using a try-finally statement without a catch clause. While this is convenient to code, my opinion is that this is a quite dangerous omission. The finally clause will execute in any case, even if a catch clause runs. If no catch clause is included, then the code running in the finally clause may have suffered some serious exception condition.

Applying Metrics to Java Version 8

At the time of writing, the Java language is at version 8. This version of Java has had some interesting additions. Let's see how one of the core language additions looks under the metrics microscope. The Java 8 feature we'll look at next is that of Lambdas as illustrated in Listing 3.

Can you make any sense of Listing 3?

```
Listing 3 - Java 8 Code Using Lambdas
public static void main(String... args) {
  Calculator myApp = new Calculator();
  IntegerMath addition = (a, b) -> a + b;
  IntegerMath subtraction = (a, b) -> a - b;
  RealMath division = (a, b) -> a / b;
  System.out.println("137 / 12 = " +
    myApp.operateBinary(137, 2, division));
  System.out.println("40 + 2 = " +
    myApp.operateBinary(40, 2, addition));
  System.out.println("20 - 10 = " +
```

```
myApp.operateBinary(20, 10, subtraction));
}
```

As usual, let's apply the metrics to the Java 8 code. Again, as usual here is the list of metrics.

1. Variable names that are too short and provide no usage context
2. Code that provides no context or obvious purpose
3. Inconsistent spacing
4. Inconsistent parameter type definition
5. Incomprehensible code
6. Code that is too long
7. No exception handling
8. No automatic resource management
9. External calls that are not contained in separate methods
10. Inadequate abstraction - need for higher level code
11. Code that is difficult or impossible to change

The code in Listing 3 is actually pretty profound! It uses a technique generally available only in C (function pointers) and **in functional programming languages**. What technique is that? Well, it's the advanced feature of passing code as data. In effect, this allows code to be passed into a method as a parameter. This occurs in the line: myApp.operateBinary(20, 10, subtraction) and in the other two invocations of myApp.operateBinary().

Once we have this vital piece of information, the code in Listing 3 becomes much easier to understand. So, the metrics analysis is then as follows:

1. Variable names that are too short and provide no usage context - **needs attention**
2. Code that provides no context or obvious purpose - **needs attention - add comments**
3. Inconsistent spacing - **no change needed**
4. Inconsistent parameter type definition - **no change needed**

5. Incomprehensible code - **needs attention - add comments**
6. Code that is too long - **no change needed**
7. No exception handling - **no change needed**
8. No automatic resource management - **no change needed**
9. External calls that are not contained in separate methods - **no change needed**
10. Inadequate abstraction - need for higher level code - **no change needed**
11. Code that is difficult or impossible to change - **no change needed**

Listing 4 illustrates the code after applying the metrics.

Listing 4 - Post-metric Java 8 Code Using Lambdas

```
public static void main(String... args) {
  Calculator myApp = new Calculator();
  // Lambda to be used for functional call
  IntegerMath addition = (argumentA, argumentB) ->
argumentA + argumentB;
  IntegerMath subtraction = (argumentA, argumentB) ->
argumentA - argumentB;
  RealMath division = (argumentA, argumentB) ->
argumentA / argumentB;
  System.out.println("137 / 12 = " +
    myApp.operateBinary(137, 2, division));
  System.out.println("40 + 2 = " +
    myApp.operateBinary(40, 2, addition));
  System.out.println("20 - 10 = " +
    myApp.operateBinary(20, 10, subtraction));
}
```

One could also argue the case for putting in some division by zero protection in the method `division`. Also, the use of hardcoded numbers is not a great idea, but is used for illustration. These values should be passed in as parameters or coded as constants.

I think the code in Listing 4 is now easier to understand and modify. The use of the word Lambda in the comment has provided a clue to the code maintainer that the code contains a Java 8 Lambda function. Of course, as the users of Java start to routinely employ Lambdas, the need for comments will diminish. The point here is that if you use a new feature of a language, then it may make sense to put in a note to help the downstream users of your code.

Applying the Metrics Approach To Java Concurrency Code

Let's now apply a metrics analysis to one of the most demanding areas of programming: concurrency management. The rapid proliferation of multi-core platforms and devices has made knowledge of concurrent programming a mandatory addition to the programming toolkit. Listing 5 illustrates a common concurrency pattern called a **critical section**.

Listing 5 - Java Concurrency Code - Critical Section
```java
public int applyLock() {
  boolean tryLockResult = true;

  try {
    tryLockResult = getInventoryLock().tryLock();
    System.out.println("Result of tryLock() is " +
tryLockResult);
    setCountValue(getCountValue() + 1);
  } catch (Exception e) {
    e.printStackTrace();
  } finally {
    getInventoryLock().unlock();
  }

  if (!tryLockResult) {
    System.out.println("**** Got a lock false result");
  }
  return getCountValue();
```

`}`

A critical section is a piece of code that exists to protect access to a shared resource. Only one thread at a time is allowed access to the critical section. In the case of Listing 5, the critical section increments a shared integer value in the line
`setCountValue(getCountValue() + 1)`. Each client thread requests a new value and the value returned must be unique. In the case of Listing 5, the underlying type of the lock is a Java ReentrantLock.

There is an issue with the Listing 5 code, and it's at the beginning. Notice the call to
`getInventoryLock().tryLock()`. This code attempts to apply a lock, which is what we need. But, the difficulty is that
`getInventoryLock().tryLock()` returns immediately, regardless of whether or not the lock has been applied. In fact, the result of the lock is communicated in the boolean return value of
`getInventoryLock().tryLock()`. A true value indicates the lock was obtained and a false value indicates failure. The latter occurs when some other competing thread got into the critical section first.

So, let's see how the metrics analysis works out.

1. Variable names that are too short and provide no usage context
2. Code that provides no context or obvious purpose
3. Inconsistent spacing
4. Inconsistent parameter type definition
5. Incomprehensible code
6. Code that is too long
7. No exception handling - **needs attention**
8. No automatic resource management
9. External calls that are not contained in separate methods
10. Inadequate abstraction - need for higher level code
11. Code that is difficult or impossible to change

The critical section is implemented in the try-finally block in Listing 5. However, even though we have a full try-catch-finally block, the code is not equipped to handle all concurrency demands. This is because the `getInventoryLock().tryLock()` returns in all cases, including when the lock is not applied. So, the code in Listing 5 is too optimistic.

Listing 6 - Java Concurrency Code - Critical Section
```
public int applyLock() {
  try {
    getInventoryLock().lock();
    setCountValue(getCountValue() + 1);
  } catch (Exception e) {
    e.printStackTrace();
  } finally {
    getInventoryLock().unlock();
  }

  return getCountValue();
}
```

Listing 6 is now much shorter than Listing 5. The critical section now waits its turn to increment the shared count variable.

Chapter Summary

Even very well-structured and well-designed Java code can benefit from a metrics analysis. The examples in this chapter are of reasonably good quality code. However, even such code can be difficult for a non-expert reader.

Not including a catch clause is a poor practice, which makes the code less able to handle unanticipated exceptions. Given that a try-finally block was already written in Listing 1, adding a catch clause seems like plain common sense. In other words, just a few minor changes can make all the difference between complex and brittle code. All driven by metrics.

In Listing 3, we saw one of the new language features in Java 8. It is entirely possible that a downstream developer or a code maintainer may not be familiar with this language feature. Adding a simple comment and some meaningful variable names is a small investment in helping other users to understand the code.

Concurrency programming is a difficult area to master. However, the wide availability of multicore platforms makes a solid knowledge of concurrency programming a mandatory requirement. What makes concurrency so difficult is the fact that code can run successfully during development but then fail under production loading. Again, a metrics analysis can help to uncover even the most difficult concurrency problems.

Chapter 5 Using Code Quality Metrics To Refactor C++

Let's now look at metrics use in understanding and refactoring another mainstream high level language: C++. The examples used in this chapter incorporate the area of both concurrent and asynchronous coding. We saw some Java concurrency code in the previous chapter. Just as is the case for concurrency coding, asynchronous code development is traditionally a quite difficult topic. In a nutshell, asynchronous coding allows you to make calls to external code (such as a function) and then expect the results to come back at some future time. The asynchronous mechanism allows you to govern the manner in which you wait for the results. Typically, your code can do other work while waiting or it can do no work and just wait.

In the past, complex mechanisms were often required for asynchronous programming. Fortunately, C++ version 11 now includes standard features to support asynchronous development. Let's have a look at some code!

Promise-Future C++ Asynchronous Code

Given the widespread availability of multi-processor machines, the need for asynchronous development skills is growing. With this in mind, have a look at Listing 1 and see can you figure out what's going on.

Note: In the following examples, I use embedded numbers in the code. This is generally not good practice, rather I should use symbolic constants, which is the preferred practice. I use embedded numbers or magic numbers just to keep the code a little shorter and hopefully easier to follow.

Listing 1 - C++ Asynchronous Code

```cpp
void accessPromise (std::future<int>& fut) {
  int x = fut.get();
  std::cout << "Just got promised value: " << x <<
'\n';
}

int main() {
  std::promise<int> prom;
  std::future<int> fut = prom.get_future();
  std::thread th1 (accessPromise, std::ref(fut));
  prom.set_value (20);
  th1.join();
  sleep(5);
```

In Listing 1, we have three major code elements: promise, future, and thread. It turns out that this is a standard synchronization pattern. Looking at the code in Listing 1, it just takes a little bit of Googling to find out that the promise-future pattern is being used. This pattern also typically uses a delay component. Armed with this information, it's then not so difficult to understand the Listing 1 code.

Basically, a promise is being created (or made) to provide some data for use in the future. To model this, the promise is tied into what is called a future object. The future is then associated with a thread of execution. Next, the promise value is set and this is then accessed through the future object as part of the thread execution context.

Listing 2 illustrates an example run of the code from Listing 1.

```
Just got promised value: 20
```

Nothing too surprising there. The promised value is delivered to the thread thanks to the synchronization mechanism. Let's now see how the code in Listing 1 stands up to a metrics analysis. Here's my take on how the code stacks up against the metrics.

1. Variable names that are too short and provide no usage context - **needs attention**
2. Code that provides no context or obvious purpose
3. Inconsistent spacing
4. Inconsistent parameter type definition
5. Incomprehensible code
6. Code that is too long
7. No exception handling - **needs attention**
8. No automatic resource management
9. External calls that are not contained in separate methods
10. Inadequate abstraction - need for higher level code - **needs attention**
11. Code that is difficult or impossible to change

Metrics 1, 7, and 10 suggest to me that the code needs some attention.

Metric 1 - Variable name size

The choice of a variable name for the future object is quite important. So, a little bit more context might enhance the code readability. With this in mind, I would suggest that the variable names `prom` and `fut` could be replaced with something like this: `valuePromise` and `futureState`. Also, the function name `accessPromise` might be easier to understand if it was changed to `accessPromisedValue`. The last suggestion would be to use a longer variable name than `x`.

As C++ programmers become more conversant with patterns such as promise-future, the need for comments will diminish. But, before widespread understanding is the norm, it may be prudent to spell things out a little more to assist downstream developers.

Metric 7 - Exception Management

My second major objection to the Listing 1 code relates to exception management. One of the key things about the promise-future pattern is the fact that it facilitates shared state, i.e., shared data between the promise and future objects. This data can become invalid and this should be reflected in the function that retrieves the state data.

Metric 10 - Line Ending

Notice in Listing 1, the line ending is: '\n'. This can instead be replaced with the C++ symbol: endl. One benefit of the endl symbol is that the output buffer is flushed (assuming this is required). This can be useful during program development, for example, when the code may not be fully stable. If the file data is for code logging, then it may be useful to ensure that flushing occurs.

Listing 2 illustrates the modified code after the metrics analysis.

Listing 2 - C++ Asynchronous Code After Metrics Analysis
```
void accessPromise (std::future<int>& futureState) {
  int promisedValue = 0;

  if(futureState.valid()) {
    promisedValue = futureState.get();
```

```
      std::cout << "Just got promised value: " <<
promisedValue << endl;
   } else {
      std::cout << "Future data is invalid" << endl;
   }
}

int main() {
   std::promise<int> valuePromise;
   std::future<int>  futureState =
valuePromise.get_future();
   cout << "Future validity " <<  futureState.valid() <<
endl;
   std::thread th1 (accessPromise,
std::ref(futureState));
   valuePromise.set_value (20);
   th1.join();
   sleep(5);
   cout << "Future validity " << futureState.valid() <<
endl;
   return 0;
}
```

Running the code in Listing 2 produces the following output:

```
Future validity 1
Just got promised value: 20
Future validity 0
```

Notice the way the future state is valid (i.e., state is true) before the promised value is retrieved. Then, when the future value is acquired, the promise has been fulfilled and the latter is then no longer valid. The difference between Listings 1 and 2 is clarity and comprehensibility. Was it worth doing a metric analysis? I think it was worth the effort.

Straight C++ Asynchronous Code

Here's another example of C++ asynchronous code in Listing 3. Armed with the knowledge gleaned from Listings 1 and 2, see if you can figure it out and also see what metric-related improvements you might make.

Listing 3 - Another C++ Asynchronous Code Example
```cpp
bool testValue (int x) {
  std::cout << "Calculating. Please, wait...\n";
  if (x%2==0) {
    return true;
  } else {
    return false;
  }
}

int main() {
  std::future<bool> aFuture=std::async
(testValue,3524353513222313);
  bool ret=aFuture.get();
  if (ret) {
    std::cout << "Value is even\n";
  } else {
    std::cout << "Value is not even\n";
  }
  return 0;
}
```

As usual, here's my take on how the code stacks up against the metrics.

1. Variable names that are too short and provide no usage context
2. Code that provides no context or obvious purpose - **needs attention**
3. Inconsistent spacing - **needs attention**
4. Inconsistent parameter type definition
5. Incomprehensible code
6. Code that is too long
7. No exception handling - **needs attention**

8. No automatic resource management
9. External calls that are not contained in separate methods
10. Inadequate abstraction - need for higher level code
11. Code that is difficult or impossible to change

Metric 2 - Function name is unclear

In Listing 3, the function name for checking the value is not too clear. In the interests of clarity, a better name than `testValue` might be `isValueEven`. One merit of the latter is that the purpose of the function call is obvious when reading the main function. This is an example of the benefits of comprehensible code in helping other readers to understand code!

Metric 3 - Inconsistent Spacing

The code could become clearer with slightly better spacing, e.g., changing
```
ret=aFuture.get();
```
to
```
ret = aFuture.get();
```

Metric 7 - Exception Management

As in the previous example, the data item passed to the future should be given a validity check. It's generally prudent to verify data validity in order to avoid surprises, such as, corrupted data.

Listing 4 illustrates the modified C++ code after the metrics analysis.

Listing 4 - C++ Asynchronous Code After Metrics Analysis

```cpp
bool isValueEven (int x) {
  std::cout << "Calculating. Please, wait..." << endl;
  if (x % 2 == 0) {
    return true;
  } else {
    return false;
  }
}

int main() {
  std::cout << "Checking whether 3524353513222313 is
even." << endl;
  std::cout << "Value of validity is: " <<
aFuture.valid() << endl;
  bool ret = false;

  if(aFuture.valid()) {
    ret = aFuture.get();
    if (ret) {
      std::cout << "Value is even" << endl;
    } else {
      std::cout << "Value is not even" << endl;
    }
  } else {
    std::cout << "Invalid incoming data" << endl;
  }

  return 0;
}
```

Following the metrics analysis, there's a definite improvement in the clarity and safety of the code. It's safer because the data value is being checked for validity.

Let's now look at another C++ example in the thorny area of resource management. As we've seen in many previous examples, resource management is an area where a great many programming errors occur.

C++ Version 11 Automatic Resource Management

Have a look at the C++ code in Listing 5. See can you spot any issues.

Listing 5 - C++ Object Allocation Issue
```cpp
Person *createPerson(string name)
{
  Person *p = new Person(name, 100);
  cout << "Person just created is: " << p->getName() <<
endl;
  return p;
}

void getPersonDetails(string name)
{
  Person* person = createPerson(name);
  cout << "Person name = " << person->getName();
}

int main() {
  getPersonDetails("John");

  return 0;
}
```

In Listing 5, we instantiate an object of a class called `Person`. The details of the class are not so important to the discussion. What is important is the fact that the code calls the C++ `new` operator. Let's now review the code using the metrics.

1. Variable names that are too short and provide no usage context
2. Code that provides no context or obvious purpose
3. Inconsistent spacing
4. Inconsistent parameter type definition
5. Incomprehensible code
6. Code that is too long

7. No exception handling - **needs attention**
8. No automatic resource management - **needs attention**
9. External calls that are not contained in separate methods
10. Inadequate abstraction - need for higher level code
11. Code that is difficult or impossible to change

Metric 7 - Exception Management

It's always worth remembering that any call to `new()` can fail if insufficient heap memory is available for the allocation. The default case in such a situation is for a `bad_alloc` exception to be thrown. If no handler is available to catch this exception, then the program will terminate. Of course, the difficulty here is that the exception might never occur if memory allocation is being managed correctly. But, it is always prudent to assume that error conditions will eventually present themselves in your code. It's even more prudent to plan for handling the errors!

With this in mind, two strategies are possible in relation to problems with the `new()`. The first is to simply surround all calls to `new()` with a try-catch block as in:

```
try {
   Person *p = new Person(name, 100);
}
catch (const std::bad_alloc&) {
   cout << "Received bad_alloc" << endl;
   // Do something with this exception
}
```

If we wanted to use this approach, then an updated version of the `createPerson()` function might be something like Listing 6.

Listing 6 - A Modified Object Allocation Function
```
Person* createPerson(string name)
```

```
{
  Person *p = NULL;

  try {
    p = new Person(name, 100);
    cout << "Person just created is: " << p->getName()
<< endl;
  } catch (const std::bad_alloc&) {
    cout << "Error received bad_alloc" << endl;
    // Do something with this exception
  }

  return p;
}
```

In Listing 6, if we get a bad_alloc exception, then the function will return a NULL pointer. Client code must then take account of the fact that a NULL pointer has been returned. So, this is one solution.

A lot of C++ programmers don't like using exceptions. Why so? Well, exception management is not a free technology. It requires additional code to handle exceptions and this can affect performance. So, C++ provides another mechanism for memory allocation errors, where a NULL pointer is returned if a call to new() fails. How do we use this second mechanism?

Listing 7 - Another Modified Object Allocation Function
```
Person* createPerson(string name)
{
  Person *p = NULL;

  p = new (std::nothrow) Person(name, 100);
  if (p == NULL) {
    cout << "Error received bad_alloc" << endl;
  } else {
    cout << "Person just created is: " << p->getName()
<< endl;
    }

  return p;
}
```

Listing 7 is the alternative technique for handling allocation errors. The last metric issue is in relation to resource management.

Metric 8 - Automatic Resource Management

Listing 5 has a memory leak in the following function:

```
void getPersonDetails(string name)
{
  Person* person = createPerson(name);
  cout << "Person name = " << person->getName();
}
```

The problem is that there is no corresponding call to delete. So, the allocated memory is said to leak. This is so much of a problem in legacy C++ code that a new mechanism has been added to version 11 of the language. This mechanism is called Resource Acquisition Is Initialization or RAII. How does RAII work? Well, in this case it works by using what are called unique pointers.

Listing 8 illustrates an updated version of Listing 5 using a unique pointer. Can you figure out the difference between Listings 5 and 8?

Listing 8 - Using C++ Version 11 RAII
```
unique_ptr<Person> createPersonRAII(string name)
{
  unique_ptr<Person> p(new(std::nothrow) Person(name,
100));
  if (p != NULL) {
    cout << "Person just created is: " << p-<getName()
<< endl;
    return p;
  } else {
    return NULL;
  }
}
```

```
void getPersonDetails()
{
   unique_ptr<Person> person = createPersonRAII("Mary");
   cout << "Person name = " << person->getName(); // Get
the person's name
   // The person object is now destroyed on exit
}

int main() {
   getPersonDetails();

   return 0;
}
```

So, what's so different about the code in Listing 8? Well, in a nutshell, once the `person` object goes out of scope, its destructor is called and any memory allocated is returned to the free pool. This is automatic resource management in action. In fact, when you think about it, RAII is a replacement for the `finally` clause in the `try-catch` statement. It helps to simplify C++ coding and also to avoid an all too common class of error (i.e., resource leakage).

Chapter Summary

Metrics-driven programming is just as applicable to C++ as it is to the other languages we've reviewed. One of the biggest (if not the biggest) challenges in designing and building concurrent C++ applications is state management. The promise-future model of C++ asynchronous coding provides a powerful mechanism for communicating state between code elements. In addition, the state or data communicated is protected and can be verified before use. This potentially makes for more survivable asynchronous C++ solutions.

Metrics analysis of C++ also allows for more solid exception handling. This is helped by the fact that C++ provides two distinct exception philosophies. In this way, the requirements of the various language users continue to be fulfilled as C++ evolves.

As in previous chapters, issues related to resource management continue to challenge modern programmers. The metrics approach allows for uncovering subtle resource issues and C++ version 11 provides excellent facilities to help the programmer. One such facility is RAII.

In all of the above cases, a metrics-based approach assists in producing better code.

Chapter 6 Case study - Implementing a design pattern for telecoms

The singleton as a network management pattern

In this chapter, I implement a much larger amount of code than has been seen in the book. This is an exercise that allows us to see the way requirements can be mapped from design into working code. The requirements address both functional end-user needs as well as what are often called non-functional needs. The latter includes the use of a standard design pattern.

In the case study that follows, I'll be delving into a little more jargon than usual. This jargon relates to the telecoms domain from which the case study is derived. It's pretty standard for every industry to have its very own set of arcane terms and expressions. An important part of designing and building software solutions is having a solid understanding of the domain in question. So, the approach I generally use is to try to get an overview, i.e., learn as much as is required to get started and then dig in deeper later on. One might say, that learning an organizational domain is somewhat akin to learning to read code!

Before getting started, let's look at some background detail.

Service-driven networking

Service-driven networking requires rapid automated provisioning in response to user demand. Suppose you want to increase your allocated home broadband bandwidth. Typically, to upgrade your bandwidth, you'll fill in an online order form or speak to a customer service representative. This will eventually result in a **provisioning server** updating your connection profile. Some time after this, your broadband link will be upgraded. Service providers are falling over themselves to achieve this type of customer response. Indeed, in some countries, where optical fibre is being deployed nationally, the speed upgrade is often free and requires no customer input. In short, speed and accuracy of order fulfilment is of the essence.

An important element of this is the provisioning server - the software that modifies the network to deliver the requested service upgrade. In particular, I'll look at how to use the Singleton design pattern, among others, to implement a simple, single-instance, extensible provisioning server. The provisioning server will be used to modify the bandwidth of the service provider link for two types of users: a home office user, and a large enterprise network.

Software design patterns

As we've seen in earlier chapters, design patterns such as, separation of concerns, can greatly improve code legibility. This helps to facilitate downstream comprehension and modification of code.

The other major merit of using patterns is the speed at which fairly complex and complete software can be written. In terms of software abstraction, patterns also encourage architects, designers, and developers to think outside the box (i.e., outside the code) by sharing a common vocabulary. A simple example of this is when an architect or designer says that: "Class X should be loosely coupled to class Y because Y will likely change in future releases". The developers can then create the two classes so that X and Y are minimally co-dependent, e.g., incorporating the facade pattern. Also, defining class interfaces can help provide another boost to loose coupling. This is a pattern example that can help in reducing unnecessary future code changes.

One of the best investments of our precious time is to study design patterns in your primary programming language. Then, as you read the pattern examples, try to dream up applications (in your own specific domain) for each of the different pattern variants. This is a difficult undertaking but potentially very rewarding. Because, later when you're embroiled in a project and trying to solve tough problems, you can consult your patterns notes to see when/if a pattern can be employed. This is also often a good time to update your notes. Used in this way, patterns help move developers up the value chain.

Service With a Smile

Our goal here is to be able to quickly switch on or upgrade an existing network service. To do this, we must interact with the network and change its configuration and state in some fashion. In this particular case, we will be allocating more bandwidth from a service provider. This simple task is often incredibly difficult to achieve in telecoms networks! It requires interaction with multiple back end systems - service portals, databases, and network devices, as illustrated in Figure 1.

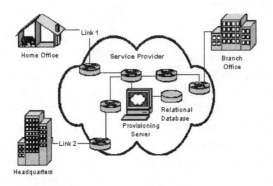

Figure 1: Service Provider Network Layers

In spite of the complexity, there is a growing demand for customer-driven network management. One reason why telecoms is especially complex is because of its intrinsically 3-tier nature - users, back end systems (Provisioning Server and database), and network devices (routers and switches) as illustrated in Figure 1. Let's now take a quick look at the typical workflows that accompany the user-driven service change requests.

Sample Workflow

The home office user in Figure 1 places an online order for an increase in the bandwidth of her broadband connection (Link 1 in Figure 1). Likewise, the network manager at the Headquarters site also places an order to increase the bandwidth on Link 2. These two orders are typically routed through some type of workflow system (not shown in Figure 1) that verifies the change requests. The change requests are ultimately translated into a series of device configuration changes that are applied in an orderly fashion to the routers and switches (the hockey puck symbols) in Figure 1.

We'll simulate this workflow with a simple user-driven GUI front end that communicates with the Provisioning Server in Figure 1. This GUI is typically accessed using a browser. The Provisioning Server then applies the required changes to the backend systems (in this case, storing the request in a database) and updating the associated network devices.

In the midst of all this complexity, we want to provide a way to rapidly implement the required capability. Patterns come to the rescue! Let's briefly review the major requirements:

- The user interface allows limited service display and change requests
- A single instance of a provisioning server handles all change requests
- The provisioning server updates the backend systems, i.e., the database(s) and network devices

So, we need a basic GUI for the customers in Figure 1. This GUI facility is often called customer network management and is increasingly a feature of service provider networks. A very popular customer network management feature is called service level assurance monitoring. This allows a customer to view the parameters of a contractual service level agreement (e.g., 100Mbps guaranteed, round trip delay 20ms, etc.). If the customer breaks the agreement by sending too much traffic, then the provider can drop excess traffic. If the service provider fails to meet the agreement (e.g., dropping or delaying traffic during periods of congestion), then the customer may get a financial rebate. Creating the infrastructure to do this is a key part of modern network management.

So, our provisioning server in Figure 1 handles all service change requests and typically routes them for validation to other systems. This offloading helps reduce the load on the provisioning server.

The provisioning server focuses its efforts on presenting a single instance, receiving orders, and updating the complex backend systems. For this reason, it's a good candidate for implementation using the Singleton pattern. So, now that we have a handle on the domain requirements, let's take a look at the Singleton pattern.

The Singleton Pattern

Singleton is often used in situations where you want just one (and only one) instance of a class in a given Java Virtual Machine. This can be useful for applications that require a single point of entry for a block of functionality, e.g., order fulfilment in our example domain. In the telecoms world, it's often generally important to have a strict ordering on the use of devices, such as routers or legacy network elements.

By ordering, I mean configuration commands are sent at a predetermined rate of arrival so as not to overwhelm the device. In many cases, the devices implement network management facilities in code that has a lower priority than the traffic handling code. Remember, network devices have a lot of work to do besides responding to network management commands - all the more so, as network technology speeds and feeds increase.

In effect, resource consumption can be controlled using the Singleton pattern. Let's now have a look at a simple front end for placing orders.

The Service Order GUI

The service order GUI is very simple - it allows the user to see and update the existing configuration of their service. For our home office user, this is 100Mbps on Link1 in Figure 1 and for the corporate user it's 500Mbps on Link 2 in Figure 1. In passing, please note that the units of kilo- and mega- in the telecoms world relate to 1000 and 1,000,000 respectively (not 1024 and 1,048,576 as used in the domain of disk storage). So, 100Mbps is actually 100,000,000bps and 500Mbps is 500,000,000bps.

Let's assume our home office user wins the lottery and decides to upgrade her connection by 100Mbps. She runs the service configuration program and sees the GUI shown in Figure 2. This is the allowed view of the service for our newly rich home office user!

Figure 2 Home User Service Configuration View

The current allocated service level is 100Mbps and three options are available with the portal in Figure 2:

- Update Profile - allows the configuration to be changed
- Undo - reverses the most recent configuration change
- Exit - exit the program

Selecting the update profile option results in sending an order to the provisioning server to upgrade the service by 100Mbps as illustrated in Figure 3.

Figure 3 Home Office User Service Update View

It's very similar when the enterprise user requests a service update as illustrated in Figure 4. As for the home user, the order is dispatched to the server and applied to

the network.

Figure 4 Enterprise User Service Configuration View

Notice the options in Figures 2, 3, and 4 to update and

undo the operation. This is an example of another design pattern called Command. The purpose of command pattern is to support undo capability, which is useful if the user makes a mistake or decides to apply another replacement action.

The Provisioning Server

The Provisioning Server is implemented as a single class using the singleton pattern. The main element is a list collection into which GUI orders are placed. In a production system, the server might be implemented as an RMI (or CORBA) endpoint. The implementation here is much simpler but allows for extension. The key element is the use of the singleton pattern. The server class provides a private constructor and maintains a private static instance of itself.

The server offers four public methods to clients:

1. getInstance()
2. executeCommand()
3. undoCommand()
4. toString()

The getInstance() method returns a reference to the provisioning server singleton class. The client can use this to call the other public methods as described below.

The executeCommand() method dispatches an order (formed via the GUI) to the server. This order takes the form of a textual message that includes the operation count, the user ID, and the order details. Orders are appended to an operations list object. The server could store these details in the database (via JDBC or using ORM) and then apply the required updates to the network devices (via SNMP or some other device access technology).

The undoCommand() reverses the most recent order submitted by the associated GUI client. An important part of this is that the orders from the user types are not mixed up. If the enterprise network manager decides to reverse an order, then it's essential that this has no effect on the home office user.

The toString() method returns a string representation of the operations list for a specific user. In this program, we have two possible users: "Home Office User" and "Enterprise User" respectively.

The Java Code

Three Java classes make up the code base in this example:

- RunPattern.java
- ServicePortal.java
- ProvServer.java

RunPattern.java executes the software. It opens with a brief description of the program. Next, two GUI user instances are created, i.e., Figures 2 and 4 respectively. The associated users can then interact with their GUIs and update their service provider link as required. A production system would package this differently, perhaps as a Web service or some type of online portal.

```
public class RunPattern {
    public static void main(String [] arguments) {
    System.out.println(" This program illustrates the
use of the Singleton pattern");
    System.out.println(" by creating two GUI-based
clients. These clients submit");
    System.out.println(" operation requests to the
single instance of a provisioning");
    System.out.println(" server. The latter is
implemented as a Singleton. The requests");
    System.out.println(" are actioned by the
provisioning server. Each client");
    System.out.println(" can view the changes it has
made to the provisioning server");
    System.out.println(" operations list.");
    System.out.println("Creating the first GUI
portal");
    System.out.println();
    ServicePortal portal1 = new ServicePortal();
```

```
    portal1.createUserView("Home Office User",
"Service - 100Mbps link");
    System.out.println("Creating the second GUI
portal");
    System.out.println()
    ServicePortal portal2 = new ServicePortal();
    portal2.createUserView("Enterprise User",
"Service - 500Mbps link");
    }
}
```

ServicePortal.java

The ServicePortal class provides a simple Swing GUI
that is coupled to the ProvServer class. The buttons on
the GUI provide access to the appropriate methods in the
latter.

```java
import java.awt.Container;
import javax.swing.BoxLayout;
import javax.swing.JButton;
import javax.swing.JFrame;
import javax.swing.JPanel;
import javax.swing.JTextArea;
import java.awt.event.ActionEvent;
import java.awt.event.ActionListener;
import java.awt.event.WindowAdapter;
import java.awt.event.WindowEvent;

public class ServicePortal implements ActionListener {
    private JFrame mainFrame;
    private JTextArea textDisplay;
    private JButton updateService, undoButton,
exitButton;
    private JPanel controlPanel, displayPanel;
    private static int operationCount;
    private String userId;

    public void createUserView(String userName, String
serviceDescription) {
        userId = userName;
        mainFrame = new JFrame("Provisioning Server as
Singleton");
```

```
        Container content = mainFrame.getContentPane();
        content.setLayout(new BoxLayout(content,
BoxLayout.Y_AXIS));
        displayPanel = new JPanel();
        textDisplay = new JTextArea(20, 60);
        textDisplay.setEditable(false);
        textDisplay.setText(userName + ". " +
serviceDescription);
        displayPanel.add(textDisplay);
        content.add(displayPanel);
        controlPanel = new JPanel();
        updateService = new JButton("Update Profile");
        undoButton = new JButton("Undo");
        exitButton = new JButton("Exit");
        controlPanel.add(updateService);
        controlPanel.add(undoButton);
        controlPanel.add(exitButton);
        content.add(controlPanel);
        updateService.addActionListener(this);
        undoButton.addActionListener(this);
        exitButton.addActionListener(this);
        mainFrame.addWindowListener(new
WindowCloseManager());
        mainFrame.pack();
        mainFrame.setVisible(true);
    }

    public void refreshTextDisplay() {
        textDisplay.setText("Provisioning Server Command
History for " + userId +"\n" +
            ProvServer.getInstance().toString(userId));
    }

    public void actionPerformed(ActionEvent evt) {
        Object originator = evt.getSource();
        if (originator == updateService) {
            executeCommand(" " + userId + " Increase
bandwidth by 100Mbps");
        } else if (originator == undoButton) {
            undoCommand();
            } else if (originator == exitButton) {
                exitApplication();
            }
    }

    private class WindowCloseManager extends
WindowAdapter {
```

```java
        public void windowClosing(WindowEvent evt) {
            exitApplication();
        }
    }

    private void executeCommand(String message) {
ProvServer.getInstance().executeCommand((++operationCou
nt) + message);
        refreshTextDisplay();
    }

    private void undoCommand() {
        Object result =
ProvServer.getInstance().undoCommand(userId);

        if (operationCount > 0)
          operationCount--;

        refreshTextDisplay();
    }

    private void exitApplication() {
        System.exit(0);
    }
}
```

ProvServer.java

The ProvServer class implements the required
provisioning server. As described earlier, it has two
private data members: an operations list, and an instance
of the ProvServer class. Clients access the methods via
the getInstance() method.

```java
import java.util.ArrayList;
import java.util.Collections;
import java.util.List;
public class ProvServer {
    private List opList =
Collections.synchronizedList(new ArrayList());
```

```java
    private static ProvServer instance = new
ProvServer();

    private ProvServer() {
    }

    public static ProvServer getInstance() {
      return instance;
    }

    public void executeCommand(String command) {
      opList.add(command + " Operation --> " +
updateBackendSystems(command));
    }

    private String updateBackendSystems(String command)
{
      // Call into backend systems, e.g., database,
SNMP, CLI, etc.
      return "Succeeded";
    }

    public Object undoCommand(String userId) {
      if (opList.isEmpty()) {
        return opList;
      } else {
          for (int i = opList.size() - 1; i >= 0; i--)
{
            if (((String)
opList.get(i)).indexOf(userId) != -1) {
              opList.remove(i);
              return opList;
            }
          }
        }

      return opList;
    }

    public String toString(String userId) {
      StringBuffer result = new StringBuffer();

      for (int i = 0; i < opList.size(); i++) {
        if (((String) opList.get(i)).indexOf(userId) !=
-1) {
          result.append("  ");
          result.append(opList.get(i));
```

```
            result.append("\n");
        }
    }
    return result.toString();
}
}
```

Applying the Code Metrics

The above code was carefully designed and written using design patterns. Because of this, more time was available for thinking about the application specifics, rather than code infrastructure issues. As a result, I think the code is quite clean. However, just for completeness, I include a brief metrics analysis of the code. As usual, here is the metrics list.

1. Variable names that are too short and provide no usage context
2. Code that provides no context or obvious purpose
3. Inconsistent spacing
4. Inconsistent parameter type definition
5. Incomprehensible code
6. Code that is too long
7. No exception handling
8. No automatic resource management
9. External calls that are not contained in separate methods
10. Inadequate abstraction - need for higher level code
11. Code that is difficult or impossible to change

I would say that the following metrics are violated by the provisioning server Java code:

*   Incomprehensible code
*   Inadequate abstraction - need for higher level code

Incomprehensible code

The provisioning server is instantiated in a private method. This helps to ensure that just one instance is created (as per the requirements). It would be useful for at least a comment to this effect be added to this section of the `class ProvServer` code:

```
public class ProvServer {
    private List opList =
Collections.synchronizedList(new ArrayList());
    private static ProvServer instance = new
ProvServer();
```

In addition, the Swing code might be quite unfamiliar to a downstream developer. For this reason, some comments about how the GUI code works might be a useful addition.

Inadequate abstraction

Throughout the code, there is a range of embedded constants and magic numbers, e.g.,

```
textDisplay = new JTextArea(20, 60);
```

It is generally better practice to supply constants as parameters or as externally defined symbols. This facilitates downstream changes.

Chapter Summary

The singleton pattern is an excellent candidate for a class that must not be instantiated more than once. As with patterns in general, it offers a simple and elegant solution to the case at hand - a provisioning server. The relative ease with which the singleton pattern can be employed helps to free the developer to get to grips with solving the complex application domain issues. This provides a powerful combination of a solid pattern-based foundation and more time than usual to focus on application value add features. It also potentially allows for better product differentiation.

I didn't look at any of the middleware code that typically forms part of our service provisioning system. Typically, this code makes use of proprietary network device technology, such as SNMP, command line interfaces, etc. These technologies can be implemented using other Java technologies in conjunction with some of the other GoF (Gang of Four) patterns, such as, the Adapter pattern. The latter is employed to hide the complexities of technologies such as the ones mentioned.

Patterns provide fertile design-level ground for top-grade software development. By solving significant generic problems, such as, single instance control, patterns should become an indispensable tool for all software developers. They allow for rapid solutions to difficult recurring problems.

One aspect of patterns that particularly appeals to me is that their application can easily cross industry segments. In other words, if a developer makes an effort to understand and apply a wide range of patterns in their application domain, then there's a good chance that this knowledge is portable to another industry. A patterns-literate developer could (with some additional domain training) move for example from programming telecoms to finance systems.

Chapter 7 Conclusions

Five Steps to Better Programming

There is a worrying trend in the media and to a lesser extent in the IT industry to trivialise programming. This may be simply due to the massive proliferation of devices in common use.

Programming has never been easy and this remains true to the present day. In some respects, coding is now more challenging than ever, because programmers are now routinely expected to be fluent in a range of programming languages.

While a programmer might be strong in Java, they might not be so good in JavaScript. Likewise, a C++ programmer may not produce the best Java code.

Following the five steps to better programming provides a means of generically applying lessons learned from numerous languages. This allows for a non-expert in one language to produce a better effort than just hacking. If a Java programmer has to write a complex Bash script, then that script can be written in a nicely modularized fashion.

Peer review of programming can be significantly improved by using the metrics-based approach. Indeed, the metrics could potentially be coded into scripts that run in continuous build environments or scripts that run before checking code into version control.

On Errors - Coding Mistakes

Adhering to a metrics-based approach should substantially reduce simple and avoidable coding errors. This applies in particular to errors in resource allocation and de-allocation.

Coding Is NOT Design

Articulating a design is an opportunity to add capabilities when the associated cost is low. Why is design a good time to think about extra capabilities? Well, for one thing, design time changes tend to have much lower cost than post?integration. Leaving changes until later in the development cycle raises the team impact and the organizational cost of those changes.

For this reason, I think it is essential to not treat coding and design as contemporaneous activities. Even a design that is articulated in a few pages of a document can be the foundation for better code. It is all too easy to fall into the trap of premature coding. We saw this in the earlier section on **Java concurrency programming**.

Concurrency is a design-level feature

Concurrency or thread-safety is a programming area that has to be carefully designed. Many programmers rely heavily on development frameworks. The trouble is that the frameworks themselves may produce thread-unsafe code. It is far better if programmers understand concurrency requirements and can design code specifically to achieve them. Adding concurrency facilities to bad code is likely to be disappointing for everyone.

The same considerations apply to asynchronous coding. This is a design-centric area of development.

Patterns

Patterns are a hugely powerful programming ally. Large blocks of code can be allocated to standard patterns with confidence. Patterns help to avoid re-inventing the wheel. This amounts to standing on the shoulders of giants and includes patterns such as:

Appendix A: Publish-subscribe
Appendix B: Model view controller
Appendix C: Singleton
Appendix D: Template
Appendix E: Chain of responsibility
Appendix F: and so on

IDE Support

Modern IDEs, such as, Eclipse, NetBeans, and IntelliJ IDEA provide a great deal of programmer support. The code examples I've used have featured a metrics-driven refactoring approach. This ties in very well with the refactoring facilities available in the above IDEs. The same is true for the IDE code generation tools. Automation can greatly assist in producing high quality code. Such code is a gift to downstream users.

Testing

Most of the content of this book has been centred on code issues rather than testing. Testing is a crucial element in producing quality code. It goes without saying that test facilities should always be added to your coding efforts, specifically:

- Unit tests
- Functional tests

Again, the many excellent books on testing can help in conjunction with IDE support features.

www.ingramcontent.com/pod-product-compliance
Lightning Source LLC
LaVergne TN
LVHW092338060326
832902LV00008B/708